Criminological Theory

Frank P. Williams III

College of Criminal Justice
Sam Houston State University

Marilyn D. McShane

College of Criminal Justice
Sam Houston State University

D1005445

Prentice Hall, Englewood Cliffs, New Jersey 07632

Library of Congress Cataloging-in-Publication Data
WILLIAMS, FRANKLIN P.
    Criminological Theory.

    Includes bibliographies and index.
    1. Crime and Criminals.   I. McShane, Marilyn D.,
1956-   . II. Title.
HV6025.W48 1988   364.2   87-17427
ISBN 0-13-193640-9

Editorial production supervision and
    interior design: Elaine Lynch and Margaret Lepera
Cover Design: Edsal Enterprises
Manufacturing Buyer: Harry P. Baisley

 © 1988 by Prentice Hall
A Division of Simon & Schuster
Englewood Cliffs, NJ 07632

Printed in the United States of America

10 9 8 7 6 5 4 3 2 1

ISBN 0-13-193640-9

Prentice-Hall International (UK) Limited, *London*
Prentice-Hall of Australia Pty. Limited, *Sydney*
Prentice-Hall Canada Inc., *Toronto*
Prentice-Hall Hispanoamericana, S.A., *Mexico*
Prentice-Hall of India Private Limited, *New Delhi*
Prentice-Hall of Japan, Inc., *Tokyo*
Simon & Schuster Asia Pte. Ltd., *Singapore*
Editora Prentice-Hall do Brasil, Ltda., *Rio de Janeiro*

To our parents,

Dr. Pruitt and Ann Williams
and
Paul and Elaine McShane

CONTENTS

PREFACE   **ix**

1   INTRODUCTION   **1**

Introduction to Theory   2
What is Good Theory?   3
What Kinds of Theory Are There?   4
Levels of Explanation   5
Classification of Theory   7
Summary   8
Suggested Readings   8
Bibliography   9

2   THE CLASSICAL SCHOOL   **11**

Introduction   12
The Heritage of the School   12
The Perspective of the School   15
Classification of the School   17
Summary   17
Bibliography   18

3   THE POSITIVE SCHOOL   21

Introduction   22
The Heritage of the School   22
The Perspective of the School   24
Classification of the School   28
Summary   28
Bibliography   29

4   THE CHICAGO SCHOOL   33

Introduction   34
The Heritage of the School   34
Contributions of the Chicago School   36
Classification of the School   42
Summary   43
Bibliography   44

5   DIFFERENTIAL ASSOCIATION THEORY   47

Introduction   48
The Heritage of the Theory   48
The Theoretical Perspective   51
Classification of the Theory   53
Summary   54
Bibliography   55

6   ANOMIE THEORY   59

Introduction   60
The Heritage of the Theory   60
The Theoretical Perspective   62
Classification of the Theory   64
Summary   65
Bibliography   67

7   SUBCULTURE THEORIES   69

Introduction   70
The Heritage of the Theories   70
Cohen's Subculture of Delinquency   72

Cloward and Ohlin's Differential
    Opportunity Theory   75
Other Subculture Theories   78
Summary   79
Bibliography   80

8   LABELING THEORY   83

Introduction   84
The Heritage of the Theory   84
The Theoretical Perspective   86
Classification of the Theory   90
Summary   91
Bibliography   92

9   CONFLICT THEORY   95

Introduction   96
The Heritage of the Theory   96
The Theoretical Perspective   98
Classification of the Theory   102
Summary   103
Bibliography   104

10   SOCIAL CONTROL THEORY   107

Introduction   108
The Heritage of the Theory   108
The Theoretical Perspective   110
Classification of the Theory   113
Summary   114
Bibliography   115

11   SOCIAL-LEARNING THEORY   117

Introduction   118
The Heritage of the Theory   118
The Theoretical Perspective   119
Classification of the Theory   125
Summary   125
Bibliography   127

12 THE FUTURE OF CRIMINOLOGICAL THEORY 129

Introduction 130
The Heritage of Contemporary Theory 130
The Integration of Theory 133
Conclusions 133
Bibliography 134

INDEX 137

PREFACE

This is a book about the major sociological theories of crime. While there are other approaches to the study of crime, criminology has been oriented toward sociology since the 1920s. Therefore, it is designed as a textbook for undergraduate courses in criminological theory. Because of its brevity, it is also suitable as a supplementary text in general criminology courses. Although written with the undergraduate student in mind, there is much here that a graduate student will find of interest.

The purpose of this book is to provide a fully intelligible overview of each of the major criminological theories for the beginning student of theory. We believe, as a result of several years of teaching theory courses, that people grasp the individual theories better if they are somehow located in time and history. As a result, we have done three things:

First, we have incorporated a section, prior to any theoretical discussion, on both the social and intellectual heritage of the theory. This section will allow the reader to grasp what people were thinking and doing while each theory was being developed. Thereby, we hope to prepare the way for an *understanding*. rather than a rote memorization of each theory.

Second, the language used in each chapter is oriented toward the average college student, and does not presume a grasp of sociological terminology. Terms and concepts important enough to be incorporated are explained as they are introduced. For ease of reading, each chapter is quite short and is presented in uniform format.

Third, each theory is summarized in a series of major points. These "points" are intended to clarify earlier commentary and to demonstrate the logical connections among the various elements of the theory. They also serve as review material for examinations.

We have purposely excluded critical commentary on the various theories. The findings of pertinent research have also been omitted. Such materials do not necessarily enhance the first-time reader's understanding of the theory itself, and tend to be distracting. Moreover, the inclusion of critiques and research would make for a much longer book, something we do not think the beginning student of theory needs. We are also sure that the instructor will indulge in his or her own commentary throughout the course. If commentary and research evidence are desired, several sources are given at the end of the first chapter.

Finally, we welcome any feedback on the book. There are so many versions of each theory that some critical comments are inevitable. Since this is a book that is designed to be *used*, we invite readers, students, and teachers alike, to provide us with their ideas on how to make it even more useful.

A few acknowledgments are appropriate. Many of our students will find reflections of themselves here; we thank them for their comments over the years. Dennis Longmire read the final drafts and helped us to keep this book intelligible. A long list of people assisted us (most of them without knowing it) by providing hours of useful discussion or correspondence, among them Leslie Wilkins, Simon Dinitz, Al Reiss, Ron Akers, Ray Jeffery, Dorothy Bracey, Hal Pepinsky, Sud Reid, Bill Pelfrey, Robert Mutchnick, Tom Hickey, and David Gulick. Finally, our editor, Matt McNearney, provided the right blend of encouragement and concern.

Frank P. Williams III
Marilyn D. McShane

1

INTRODUCTION

INTRODUCTION TO THEORY

Most people immediately rebel when threatened with their first exposure to theory. This seems to happen because they think of theory as something abstract and not really applicable to the "real world." What they don't understand is that we all use theory; theory is part of everyday life. When you see a dark cloud in the sky and say that it is going to rain, you have just expressed a theory. To be sure, it is a relatively simple statement, but it does express the relationships among clouds in general, clouds that are dark, and the falling of drops of water from the sky. Theories can be about very simple ideas or very complex ones, depending upon the number and types of relationships expressed by them. Theories can also be concrete or abstract. We need them in order to live. Imagine what life would be like if you could never generalize about things, if every time you saw a cloud you had to get wet in order to conclude that it was going to rain. Theories, then, are really generalizations of a sort; they explain how two or more events are related to each other.

The way we express these generalizations, or think about things, depends on the form of knowledge we are using at the time. We know things through experience (often referred to as "empirical" knowledge), intuition, common sense, science, or because someone important to us (or even an important book) has told us so. The causes of crime, for instance, are assumed to be "known" by everyone. They are broken homes, lack of religion, hanging around with the wrong crowd, poor upbringing, and so forth. While you probably don't think of these explanations this way, they are all theories. At the same time, they are not good theories because they are too simplistic. If they were correct, then everyone whose life has these causes would be criminal (or delinquent) and, of course, we know that that is not true. Even more important, is the fact that such theories also imply the reverse, that is, people who are raised in a good family environment, are religious, and associate with the right people will *not* do anything criminal (or delinquent). This is not true, either, since self-report studies (Short and Nye, 1958; Reiss and Rhodes, 1961; Akers, 1964; Gold, 1970) tell us that most young people at one time or another do things that are against the law.

The problem with most of our day-to-day theories is that they are often illogical or that they are the product of selective observations. Human behavior is complex and any simplistic theory will be incorrect. Therefore, theories about crime and criminals tend to be complex theories, and are based on what we know (or in the case of older theories, what was known at the time) from research on crime and criminals. As a rule, they reflect systematic observation and careful logic.

WHAT IS GOOD THEORY?

Since there is usually more than one theory which purports to explain criminality at any given time, how do we know which one is best? In fact, how can we tell what is good theory in general? The most common answer is that a good theory is one which *can be tested* and which best *fits the evidence of research* (Blalock, 1969; Gibbs, 1972; Dubin, 1978). This makes sense because our theories are scientific and should already be based on research evidence. Unfortunately, the issue is not that simple.

Suppose, for a moment, that Einstein had lived and had proposed his theory of relativity two centuries before he did. It would not have been testable at that time, nor would the theory have fit the research evidence. Obviously, his theory would not have been a good theory at that time. Therefore, as changes in research evidence and the ability to measure and test occur, then so do the common criteria for a good theory. Approaches based on measuring and testing may be referred to as *quantitative*, as opposed to those which are *qualitative*, or substance-oriented.

It is these qualitative criteria that help us to resolve the problem of time-specific evidence. They include such factors as *logical soundness*, the *ability to make sense out of several conflicting positions*, and even the *degree to which the theory may sensitize people to things they otherwise would not see*. While these criteria are not often mentioned, they are no less important for the utility of a theory than quantitative tests.

Most theories of criminology do not do well on the criteria of empirical testing.[1] On the other hand, almost all of the theories made sense out of things that had been puzzling people before, and they sensitized criminologists to new and important ways of looking at the phenomena of crime. "Differential Association" theory, for instance, brought together the concepts of disorganized social areas and interaction in small, intimate groups and made sense out of differing crime rates among various groups of people. "Labeling" theory sensitized criminologists to the fact that "criminality" is due as much to how we react to people as it is to their personal characteristics. Neither of these theories meets the testability requirement very well, yet both were, and still are, very popular.

---

[1] Of course, the problem with "fitting" the research evidence may be as much with the way we test and measure as it is with the theory itself. This is the unspoken message in our example of Einstein's theory of relativity.

WHAT KINDS OF THEORY ARE THERE?

Some theories, as we have already noted, are more abstract than others. The most abstract can be called **macrotheories**. Macrotheories are broad in their scope and perhaps are best characterized as those which *explain social structure and its effects*. They paint a picture of the way the world works, fit the structure of society into that picture, and suggest how crime is related to that structure. Macrotheories focus on *rates* of crime (epidemiology) rather than on criminals themselves. Examples of this type are anomie and conflict theories.

Other, more concrete theories can be referred to as **microtheories**. These theories are based on the assumption that a particular way of characterizing society is best; that characterization is used directly to *explain how people become criminals* (etiology). The focus may be on specific groups of people, or on the individual; likewise, microtheories may range from purely social to psychological to biological. In any case, they tell us how people become criminal. Examples of this type of theory are social control and social learning theories.

Finally, as is the case with any classification scheme, there are theories which do not fit neatly into either of the two categories. We will call these **bridging theories**. These theories attempt to tell us *both how social structure comes about and how people become criminal*. In fact, bridging theories are often both epidemiological (explain differing rates of crime) and etiological (explain criminal behavior itself), examples of which are subculture theory and differential opportunity theory.

LEVELS OF EXPLANATION

These three general forms of theories can be further examined on the basis of their focus of explanation. What, for instance, is the theory attempting to explain: social structure in general, classes of people in society, small groups, or individual criminality? This problem is referred to as the **level of explanation** of a theory, or what the theory attempts to explain. Most theories cannot be directly compared to each other because they do not focus directly on the same subject.

Theories are often said to compete with each other in best accounting for crime and criminals. It should make sense that, in most instances, this is really not the case. Some theories explain how social events may give rise to crime in society, but do not attempt to explain how particular individuals become criminals; others do the opposite. Some explain the social factors important in creating criminality, others explain the psychological factors, yet others the internal biological factors. Further, some of the theories attempt to account for *crime* as a social phenomenon, while many focus directly on *criminals* and their behavior. Obviously, these various theories are not in competition because they apply to different levels of the crime and criminals problem.

Unfortunately, criminology has done little thus far to integrate these various explanatory levels; that is, there is no "theory of theories" which puts them all together in a coherent fashion. This problem of which level a theory is explaining has not yet been generally recognized in criminology, although some people are beginning to do so (e.g., Short, 1985). For those beginning the study of criminological theory, however, the idea of levels of explanation is crucial because it helps to make sense out of the differences among theories. A good understanding of the area each theory deals with will help you grasp what the theorists were writing about.

CLASSIFICATION OF THEORY

As if the problem of understanding the various theories were not difficult enough, attempts by various writers to group them by some simple differences have, ironically, made matters worse. Since the factors we have mentioned are not always self-evident, and because they are complex, theories can be classified in many ways. Students of criminology will read one textbook and think that they know the theories pretty well; then they look at another textbook, find theories classified differently, and end up confused. Clearly, the classification of theories has done as much as anything to muddy the theoretical waters for beginning students as well as for some of the more experienced criminologists.

Since these classifications exist, however, they must be dealt with. The more common ones usually have two mutually exclusive categories, or dichotomies. It should be noted that no classification is *real* because the world does not exist in black and white. There are many factors to consider, and the result is a forcing of theories into one category or the other when they might not fit any category very well. The end result is almost always an artificial scheme of classification (Williams, 1984).

One of the oldest of the classification schemes is **classical** and **positive**. The names come from two schools of thought in the eighteenth and nineteenth centuries. Classical theories focus on legal statutes, governmental structures, and the rights of humans. Positivist theories focus on the pathology in criminal behavior, on treatment, and on the correction of criminality within individuals.

Another common scheme is to separate theories into those of **structure** and those of **process**. Structural theories are those which focus on the way society is organized and its effect on behavior. Some of these are also referred to as *strain* theories because of their assumption that a disorganized society creates strain which leads to deviant behavior. Process theories attempt to explain how people become criminal. While it is sometimes difficult to classify theories in this scheme, the major orientation is on the starting point of the theory. As a rule, a structural theory will not emphasize the individual criminal and the processual theory will not emphasize social structure. These two forms correspond closely to the macro- and micro-theories we have already discussed.

The final major classification approach is that of **consensus** and **conflict**, sometimes referred to as the "old" and the "new" criminology (Gibbs, 1966). Consensus theories are those based on the assumption that there is agreement among people in a society. At the least, they assume that members of a society hold common values. Conflict theories, on the other hand, are based on the assumption that there is little agreement and that people hold conflicting values. Most conflict theories also take account of differences among social classes. Since any society may have agreement and conflict at the same time, the crux is not whether agreement exists, but whether it *originally* existed. A conflict theorist may discuss a society in agreement (Marx's false consciousness), or a consensus theorist may explain how conflict exists (Cohen's delinquent subculture). Thus, this scheme is somewhat like the chicken-and-egg controversy: One simply believes that either conflict or consensus is more natural to society.

Other schemes, of course, exist. Gibbons (1976) uses a system of biological, psychological, and social theories. Another common scheme is the use of various forms of sociological and social-psychological categories (Nettler, 1974; Kornhauser, 1978; Orcutt, 1983; Reid, 1985). In fact, nearly every criminology textbook offers a somewhat new twist to classifying theories.

SOCIAL CONTEXT AND THEORY

The final approach to understanding theory lies in an examination of social history. Writers commonly discuss theories in the abstract, especially in introductory textbooks. Because they do, it may seem that the theorist sits in isolation, inventing and creating his or her new theory. Nothing could be further from the truth. Just as there are people who have helped mold your thoughts and views of the world, so there are for the theorist. Indeed, it should be clear that any important influence in your life will leave its mark on the way you perceive the world. Just as you respond to the latest fads and social events, so does the theorist. In short, those who create theories are probably as susceptible as you are to influences in their lives. Criminological theorists are practicing social scientists and may be even more sensitive to social movements and trends than most of us. As a result, no theory can really be understood and appreciated until you are aware of the context in which it was created.

The context has two major forms, **social** and **intellectual**, handy terms to identify areas of influence on an individual. Social context refers to the world about us: the ways people in the society are thinking, the things they are doing, the events taking place, the fads and fashions that are popular, and even the way our society is structured. For example, right after the Second World War, it would have been difficult for people to criticize either our nation or the government; there was a general feeling of satisfaction with ourselves and a relative agreement about how good our values were. During the early 1970s, the opposite was common; people were uncertain about government, their lives, and their values. In both times, a theorist would have been affected by the events of the time and written into the theory some of the contemporary ideas (Williams, 1981).

The second form of context, the intellectual, refers to the personal influence of teachers, friends, family, and colleagues. Sometimes that influence extends to people whom the theorist has never even met; but the theorist has read their work and been impressed with what they had to say. For this reason, many people have been said to follow in the footsteps of their teachers. The major criminological theorists have undeniably done some "footstep following," but at the same time, their theories are popular at least in part because they were also creative.

SUMMARY

One commentator on social thought (Nisbet, 1966) has noted that it is possible to discuss theory in terms of specific schools (classifying periods of time), ideas or concepts themselves (such as anomie), or *dramatis personae* (the major theorists). We contend that it is necessary to look at all of these in order to appreciate and understand theory. Since any review of theories is in reality a history of social thought, a combination of factors needs to be taken into account. The ideas should be followed from theory to theory, the various classifications examined to see how they overlap and how they differ, and the contexts analyzed to gain a feel for the assumptions made by the theorists. Therefore, each of the following chapters will examine the social and intellectual context before discussing the theory. After the theoretical presentation, the classification schemes explored in this chapter will be applied to the theory.

We contend that theory is to be used, not read, memorized, and filed away for future recital. Ideas and concepts are not anyone's exclusive property; they should be rethought, reworked, and applied where needed. No one theory takes in a complete view of crime and criminals, much less a complete view of the world. For this reason theories should be merged and integrated to form new approaches to the problems before us. And theories should be flexible enough that citizens, police officers, and judges, as well as criminologists, can all use them to understand crime and criminals in our society.

SUGGESTED READINGS

For those who are interested in a more comprehensive, or in some cases an alternative, treatment of criminological theory, we suggest the following books:

DAVIS, NANETTE J. (1975). *Sociological Constructions of Deviance.* Dubuque, IA: William C. Brown.

FARRELL, RONALD A., and VICTORIA V. SWIGERT (1982). *Deviance and Social Control.* Glenview, IL: Scott Foresman.

GIBBONS, DON C. (1979). *The Criminological Enterprise: Theories and Perspectives.* Englewood Cliffs, NJ: Prentice-Hall.

_____, and JOSEPH F. JONES (1975). *The Study of Deviance: Perspective and Problems.* Englewood Cliffs, NJ: Prentice-Hall.

TAYLOR, IAN, PAUL WALTON, and JOCK YOUNG (1973). *The New Criminology: For a Social Theory of Deviance.* London: Routledge & Kegan Paul.

VOLD, GEORGE B., and THOMAS J. BERNARD (1986). *Theoretical Criminology.* 3rd ed. New York: Oxford University Press.

BIBLIOGRAPHY

AKERS, RONALD L. (1964). "Socio-economic status and delinquent behavior: a retest," *Journal of Research in Crime and Delinquency* 1: 38-46.

BLALOCK, HUBERT M. (1969). *Theory Construction.* Englewood Cliffs, NJ: Prentice-Hall.

DUBIN, ROBERT (1978). *Theory Building,* rev. ed. New York: Free Press.

GIBBONS, DON C. (1976). *Delinquent Behavior,* 2nd ed. Englewood Cliffs, NJ: Prentice-Hall.

GIBBS, JACK P. (1966). "Conceptions of deviant behavior: the old and the new," *Pacific Sociological Review* 9: 9-14.

_____ (1972). *Sociological Theory Construction.* Hinsdale, IL: Dryden.

GOLD, MARTIN (1970). *Delinquent Behavior in an American City.* Belmont, CA: Brooks Cole.

KORNHAUSER, RUTH R. (1978). *Social Sources of Delinquency.* Chicago: University of Chicago Press.

NETTLER, GWYNN (1974). *Explaining Crime.* New York: McGraw-Hill.

NISBET, ROBERT A. (1966). *The Sociological Tradition.* New York: Basic Books.

ORCUTT, JAMES D. (1983). *Analyzing Deviance.* Homewood, IL: Dorsey Press.

REID, SUE TITUS (1985). *Crime and Criminology,* 4th ed. New York: Holt, Rinehart and Winston.

REISS, ALBERT J., JR., and A. LEWIS RHODES (1961). "The distribution of juvenile delinquency in the social class structure," *American Sociological Review* 26: 720-732.

SHORT, JAMES F., JR. (1985). "The level of explanation problem in criminology," in Robert F. Meier (ed.) *Theoretical Methods in Criminology.* Beverly Hills: Sage, 51-72.

_____, and F. IVAN NYE (1958). "Extent of unrecorded juvenile delinquency: tentative conclusions," *Journal of Criminal Law, Criminology, and Police Science* 49: 296-302.

WILLIAMS, FRANK P., III (1981). "The sociology of criminological theory: paradigm or fad," in Gary F. Jensen (ed.), *Sociology of Delinquency: Current Issues.* Beverly Hills: Sage, 20-28.

_____ (1984). "The demise of the criminological imagination: a critique of recent criminology," *Justice Quarterly* 1: 91-106.

2

THE
CLASSICAL
SCHOOL

INTRODUCTION

The particular conceptions of crime and criminal justice that emerged in the eighteenth century are collectively known as the Classical School of criminology. The name derives from common references to that entire period of time as the "Classical Period." The term "criminology" is a misnomer since there was no criminology, as we now know it, until the late nineteenth century. The term is, nonetheless, commonly used because the period gave rise to some of the basic ideas for the operation of a criminal justice system and the processing of criminals.

Two writers of this period, Cesare Beccaria (1738-1794) and Jeremy Bentham (1748-1832), wrote the best known works and they are considered to have had the most influence. In their writings they opposed the arbitrary and capricious nature of the criminal justice systems of the time. They proposed that both the law and the administration of justice should be based on rationality and human rights, neither of which was then commonly applied.

Among the major ideas which descend from this Classical School are the concept of humans as free-willed, rational beings; utilitarianism (the greatest good for the greatest number); civil rights and due process of law; rules of evidence and testimony; determinate sentencing; and deterrence. C. Ray Jeffery (1956, 1972), speaking of classical criminology, emphasizes the focus on a legal definition of crime rather than on a concern with criminal behavior. In addition, both the Declaration of Independence and the United States Constitution reflect the concerns of the classical movement. Because of this, most of our law is Classical in nature.

THE HERITAGE OF THE SCHOOL

The Social Heritage

The eighteenth century was a period of major change. The old aristocracy was being called into question, both for its claims to natural superiority and for its corrupt political practices. A new and soon-to-be powerful middle class was rising from the profits of mercantilism and the beginnings of the Industrial Revolution. Societies were becoming urbanized. Traditional conceptions of property and ownership were also being disrupted. For example, enclosure movements, the practice of claiming sole use of and fencing of previously open lands, deprived the common people of what had been their traditional right—to use the land and its resources such as game and firewood. These changes placed stress on the poor and created a resentment that affected the agricultural and rural power base of the aristocracy.

At the same time, an emphasis on commonalities among people served to minimize national differences. With this, the rule of the Church and the aristocracy was seriously threatened. The rise of the Protestant ethic allowed people to expect success for hard work in this world and not in some Church-promised afterlife. Before this time, the common person simply had to accept his or her lot in life. The Protestant ethic promised that hard work would result in an improvement in one's life and led people to expect a direct connection between hard work and success.

Certain powerful families attempted to gain the support of the middle class in a relatively successful effort to establish dominance over the thrones of Europe. For instance, German nobility ruled in England, Poland, Russia, and Sweden. All of this led to the emergence of a new and highly volatile political system. The aristocracy found itself besieged by both the monarchies and the middle class, and its hold on the reins of power began to weaken.

The Classical period was, in many areas of life, a movement of great thought and expression. In close proximity to the time when people were reading Beccaria's great treatise, *On Crimes and Punishments,* J. S. Bach had composed and performed, the young Colonies were about to erupt into the American Revolution, and the Declaration of Independence, the United States Constitution and the Bill of Rights were written.

Writers of the Classical period examined not only human nature but social conditions as well. In the late 1700s John Howard wrote *The State of the Prisons of England and Wales,* Kant produced his great essay, *Metaphysics of Morals,* and Bentham introduced his *Introduction to the Principles of Morals and Legislation.* Revolutions took place in both the American Colonies and in France.

The judicial system was also marked by changes. Founded upon the religious structures of the Middle Ages, law was mainly the product of judicial interpretation and caprice (Maestro, 1942). Secret accusations, torture, and private trials were often faced by those accused; arbitrary and overly harsh sanctions were often applied to the convicted (Barnes, 1930). Generally, there were few written laws and existing law was applied primarily to those who were not of the aristocracy. In fact, law was often used as a political tool to suppress those who spoke out against the aristocracy.

The Intellectual Heritage

The prevailing ideas of the eighteenth century were those of reform. A group of philosophers called the Naturalists believed that experience and observation could determine much about the world, especially when fortified by the human ability to reason. They rebelled against the authority of the Church and emphasized that there was an order to things which was separate from religious revelation. Morals, ethics, and responsibilities became major topics of discussion. The application of science to the physical world had begun to reveal "truths," and people were certain that the same effort brought to bear on moral and political questions would yield similar fruit.

The major explanation for human behavior was **hedonism.** Basically, it was assumed that people would automatically attempt to maximize pleasure and minimize pain. The value of any pleasure or pain, according to Bentham (1789:29), would be determined by its intensity, duration and certainty. His theory of behavior became the basis for the concept of deterrence.

One of the major new philosophical viewpoints rested on the so-called natural human rights and justified the existence of government as a **social contract** between the state and its citizens (see, for instance, the work of John Locke). This justification came close to reversing the previous political belief that people existed to serve the government and, instead, made service to the people the rationale for government. Under this social contract a person surrendered to the authority of the state only the amount of freedom necessary to insure protection of the rights of other citizens. Although it was not really new, the idea of a social contract between people and their government served the needs of the new middle class.

Growing specialization in trade and industry required more services such as roads, ports, municipal services, and policing, and the government made an ideal provider of those services. The increasing secularization of society, in turn, fit in well with both the social contract conception of a rational human and the rising middle class. Secularism immediately suggested reforms in institutions, which was all to the benefit of the new classes.

Finally, an emphasis on **human dignity**, stemming from the Enlightenment, was characteristic of the period. A humanistic current of thought, chiefly from England and France, aroused the young intellectuals of the day. Those works which expressly influenced Beccaria were Montesquieu's *Spirit of the Laws* (1748) and the various pamphlets and letters of Voltaire (Maestro, 1973:17-18). In addition to Beccaria and Montesquieu, writers and thinkers such as Hume, Montaigne, Rousseau, Helvetius, and Condorcet were the new champions of the common people and produced eloquent writings glorifying *people* rather than the Church or state. With this growth of interest in humanity itself came a concern with improving social conditions, making possible the rise of the social sciences.

THE PERSPECTIVE OF THE SCHOOL

The Classical School, then, generally gave us a humanistic conception of how law and criminal justice systems should be constructed. It did not give rise to theories of criminal behavior; instead, hedonism was used as a theory of human nature and incorporated into the rationale for building legal structures. Crime and **law** were its focus, not criminal behavior. Law was to protect the rights of both society and the individual and its chief purpose was to deter criminal behavior. Therefore, Classical law emphasized moral responsibility and the duty of citizens to consider fully the consequences of behavior before they acted. This thinking, of course, required a conception of humans as possessing **free will** and a rational nature. Any individual should be able to weigh the pleasure to be gained in an illegal behavior against the punishment (pain) decreed by law and subsequently to decide against the act.

The role of punishment, according to Bentham, in itself was evil and should be used only to exclude some greater evil (1789:170). Thus, the only justification for punishment was **deterrence**. The Classical School saw two forms of deterrence: a specific or individual form, and a general or societal form. *Specific* deterrence applied to the individual who committed an offense. The idea was to apply just enough pain to offset the amount of pleasure gained from the offense. In fact, many suggested that punishments should be restricted to the same degree of pain as the degree of pleasure gained from the offense. They saw punishment in excess of this calculated amount as unnecessary, for it put the state in the position of despot. *General* deterrence, on the other hand, was to apply to other potential offenders by showing them that a punished individual would not gain from his or her offense.

The criminal justice system, according to the thought of the Classical School, should respect the **rights** of all people. Since government drew its authority from the social contract, all indiviuals were equal before the law. This meant that the operation of criminal justice had to be aboveboard, **due process** of law had to be followed, evidence had to be obtained from facts, and equality had to be maintained.   It was proposed that all punishments be specified by law, thus limiting judicial discretion.   Scholars such as Beccaria suspected judges of following personal whim and not the law when determining guilt. He wanted the discretion of judges limited and the process of conviction and sentencing fully spelled out by law.   In response to those who argued that exactly the same treatment of all offenders would result in inequities, Becarria said that some inequities would certainly result, but not the overburdening inequity of the old system (Beccaria, 1764:16).

Like Beccaria, Bentham argued against great judicial discretion, but saw the need to allow for some forms of decreased rationality among offenders. Punishments, he added, should not be inflicted if they are groundless, ineffective (i.e., administered to a person who was drunk or insane at the time of the offense), unprofitable, or needless.   Bentham, a writer trained in the law, sought the systematic organization of legal procedures. He divided offenses into classes and types, distinguishing between private and public wrongs, crimes against person and against property, and violations of trust. In addition, he created what he called the "felicific calculus," an elaborate schedule of punishments designed to take into account a combination of pleasure, pain, and mitigating circumstances.

Beccaria specifically decried the use of torture to elicit confessions and supported time limits on case preparation for both the defense and the prosecution. The swiftness of punishment was felt to be the strength of its deterrent value. Beccaria was also opposed to the imprisonment of those not yet convicted of crimes. Languishing in the filthy, disease-ridden prisons, many of the accused died even before being tried, a situation repugnant to the humanitarian as well as to the rational thinker of the time. The writings of Beccaria and John Howard, who toured the prisons and jails and described the conditions, inspired sweeping reforms of prison conditions and incarceration practices.

Finally, members of the Classical School were generally opposed to capital punishment. Beccaria argued that no citizen had the right to take his own life, and therefore, could not give this right to the state under the social contract. Capital punishment was, as a result, not part of the state's base of authority. Bentham, using a more pragmatic approach, pointed out that the possibility of capital punishment has a tendency to make members of a jury exercise leniency out of humane motives, therefore subverting the law. Using this same line of reasoning, he also thought that witnesses might perjure themselves out of the same humane motives.

The impact of the Classical School may be seen in the results of the French and American Revolutions. They both embraced the equality of people, the right to life and liberty, fairness in the administration of justice, and restrictions on the actions of the state. Criminal law in the United States is largely Classical, with its strong emphasis on individual responsibility for actions, and on due process of law. Not until the sentencing stage is there a move away from the Classical emphasis, with some sentences designed to "treat" the offender. Even here the current trend is toward a more determinate form of sentencing.

CLASSIFICATION OF THE SCHOOL

Since the Classical School was, in reality, a movement designed to reform society, it was both conflict-oriented and structural. The *conflict* classification derives from the fact that reforms were aimed at existing social arrangements. The new philosophy of the common people was in conflict with religious and economic systems, the old governmental structure, and forms of knowledge based on religious revelation.

The Classical School is classified as *structural* because it emphasizes the effect of societal institutions on people. There was no explanation of, nor true concern with, the exact process by which individuals became criminals. Instead, the concern focused on the way that governments made law and how that law affected the rights of citizens. The fact that the Classical School was interested in the legislation of criminal law and in the criminal justice system, rather than in criminal behavior, is characteristic of a fully structural approach. Indeed, since most of the "criminological" theories of the period were political theories, the Classical School was predominantly *macrotheoretical* in its orientation.

SUMMARY

The Classical School is characterized by: (1) an emphasis on free will choices and human rationality; (2) a view of behavior as hedonistic; (3) a focus on morality and responsibility; (4) a concern with political structure and the way in which government deals with its citizens; and (5) a concern for the basic rights of all people. These generic ideas and concerns, of course, were applied to criminal justice to produce concepts such as deterrence, civil rights, and due process of law; but it is the general characteristics, not the specific ones of criminal justice, that contain the essence of Classical thought.

Major Points of the School

1. People exist in a world with free will and make their own rational choices.
2. People have certain natural rights, among them life, liberty, and ownership of property.
3. Governments are created by the citizens of a state to protect these rights, and they exist as a social contract between those who govern and those who are governed.
4. Citizens give up only that portion of their natural rights that is necessary for the state to regulate society for the benefit of all.
5. In order to insure civil rights, legislators enact law which both defines the procedures by which transgressions will be handled and specifies the exact behaviors which make up those transgressions. This law specifies the process for determining guilt and the punishment to be meted out to those found guilty.
6. Crime is a transgression against the social contract; therefore crime is a moral offense against society.
7. Punishment is justified only to preserve the social contract. Therefore the purpose of punishment is to prevent future transgressions by deterring socially harmful behavior.
8. All people are equal in their rights and should be treated equally before the law.

BIBLIOGRAPHY

ATKINSON, CHARLES (1905). *Jeremy Bentham: His Life and Work.* Westport, CT: Greenwood (reprinted 1970).

BARNES, HARRY E., (1930). *The Story of Punishment: A Record of Man's Inhumanity to Man.* Boston: Stratford.

BECCARIA, BESARE (1764). *On Crimes and Punishments.* Trans. Henry Paolucci. Indianapolis: Bobbs-Merrill (reprinted 1963).

BENTHAM, JEREMY (1789). *An Introduction to the Principles of Morals and Legislation.* New York: Kegan Paul (reprinted 1948).

_____ (1830). *The Rationale of Punishment*. London: Robert Heward.

_____ (1905). *Theory of Legislation*. London: Kegan Paul.

GEIS, GILBERT (1955). "Jeremy Bentham," *Journal of Criminal Law, Criminology, and Police Science* 46: 159-71.

HOWARD, JOHN (1777). *The State of Prisons*. London: J. M. Dent and Sons (reprinted 1929).

JEFFERY, C. RAY (1956). "The structure of American criminological thinking," *Journal of Criminal Law, Criminology, and Police Science* 46: 658-72.

_____ (1972). "The historical development of criminology," in Herman Mannheim (ed.), *Pioneers in Criminology*, 2nd ed. Montclair, NJ: Patterson Smith, 458-98.

KANT, IMMANUEL (1785). *Foundations of the Metaphysics of Morals*. New York: Bobbs-Merrill (reprinted 1959).

LIVINGSTON, EDWARD (1873). *The Complete Works of Edward Livingston on Criminal Jurisprudence*. Montclair, NJ: Patterson Smith (reprinted 1968).

LOCKE, JOHN (1937). *Treatise of Civil Government and a Letter Concerning Toleration*. New York: D. Appleton-Century.

MAESTRO, MARCELLO T. (1942). *Voltaire and Beccaria as Reformers of Criminal Law*. New York: Columbia University Press.

_____ (1973). *Cesare Beccaria and the Origins of Penal Reform*. Philadelphia: Temple University Press.

MANNHEIM, HERMANN (ed.) (1972). *Pioneers in Criminology*, 2nd ed. Montclair, NJ: Patterson Smith.

MONACHESI, ELIO D. (1955). "Cesare Beccaria," *Journal of Criminal Law, Criminology, and Police Science* 46: 439-49.

MONTESQUIEU, CHARLES LOUIS DE SECONDAT (1721). *The Persian Letters*. New York: Bobbs-Merrill (reprinted 1964).

_____ (1748). *The Spirit of the Laws*. 2 vols. London: G. Bell and Sons (reprinted in English, 1878).

PHILLIPSON, COLEMAN (1923). *Three Criminal Law Reformers: Beccaria, Bentham and Romilly*. Montclair, NJ: Patterson Smith (reprinted 1972).

VOLTAIRE, FRANCOIS MARIE AROUET DE (1973). *The Selected Letters of Voltaire*. Trans. Richard A. Brooks. New York: New York University Press.

3

THE
POSITIVE
SCHOOL

INTRODUCTION

While the champions of the Classical period were writers and philosophers, the Positivists were more likely to be scientists, mathematicians, doctors, and astronomers. While the Classical reformers sought to modernize and civilize the system within which they lived, the Positivists reached out to order and explain the growing world around them. Earlier concentration on building a moral and fair system of justice and government was displaced by the scientific exploration and discovery of other aspects of life.

Although the Classicalists believed that humans possessed a rational mind and thus had free will to choose good over evil, the Positivists saw behavior as determined by its biological, psychological, and social traits. The primary characteristics of positivist criminological thought were a deterministic view of the world, a focus on criminal behavior instead of on legal issues such as rights, and the prevention of crime through the treatment and rehabilitation of offenders.

The use of scientific research techniques was common to those who studied criminals from a positivist perspective. In scientific analyses, data were collected to describe and explain different types of individuals as well as different social conditions. The theory of evolution, proposed by naturalists and anthropologists, formed a basis for the study of human behavior and, more specifically, of criminal behavior.

Most criminological texts limit their consideration of the Positive School to the work of three Italian writers and thus create confusion among students when the term positivism is applied to later and broader theories. This chapter will focus on positivism as a more general approach and will delve into the essence of what positivism *is*. In this way, one gains an understanding of positivism which is more general than the theories of a few people and goes beyond the biological emphasis usually associated with the Positive School.

THE HERITAGE OF THE SCHOOL

The Social Heritage

The years near the turn of the twentieth century were alive with invention and discovery. Science became a major tool of scholars and the world experienced a revolution in knowledge that brought countless changes to everyday life. Advanced communications put once-separate cultures in close contact. The Statue of Liberty was unveiled, the Eiffel Tower was completed, Ibsen wrote, Verdi composed, and Van Gogh painted. The automobile, the airplane, the phonograph, and electric lighting were introduced. Medicine embraced science, and researchers discovered germs and how to combat them. Freud developed psychoanalysis and Einstein pronounced his theory of relativity.

Central to the creations of the nineteenth and early twentieth centuries was the application of science to problems of everyday life. Perhaps as never before, a method of gaining knowledge was almost deified. With the great strides made by the application of science to industry, it was to be expected that those concerned with human affairs would have a vision of perfecting humanity through scientific study.

Of great importance was the transformation of the agriculturally-based aristocracies of the eighteenth century into complex, industrialized, urban societies. The French and American Revolutions helped foster a new climate in which the concerns of the Classical School could be addressed. People became less concerned with their governments than previously was the case and more attention was focused on social, rather than on political, problems. Rothman (1971:59-62), for example, points out that Americans saw crime as the product of inequities in British colonial rule and expected crime to be reduced with the institution of the new democracy. When crime rates failed to drop, Americans were forced to acknowledge that crime might have other bases in human behavior.

The Intellectual Heritage

Although some see little connection between the Classical and Positivist Schools, it was the Classical reaffirmation that people could develop and verify their own knowledge that led to the widespread use of science in the Positivist era. Among the various intellectual influences in this direction was the rise of a (positive) philosophy which underscored the importance of tested and systematized experience rather than pure speculation, or metaphysics. Humans were seen as responsible for their own destinies, and they were fully capable of adapting their own behaviors and social institutions to create the society which would fulfill those destinies.

A second important ingredient in the rise of positivist criminology was the concept of evolution which emerged even before the writing of Darwin. Evolution became a standard form of thinking about subjects, popularized to the extent that human societies were seen as evolving. Western societies represented the pinnacle of human accomplishment and all else was somehow less evolved. Criminals were viewed as individuals who were not as fully evolved as more civilized people. Savitz (1972:viii) even suggests that this evolutionary perspective contributed to the development of a racist view of criminality.

A final influence on positivist criminology was the emergence of anthropology. Still in its infancy as an academic discipline, anthropology presented evidence of other societies as being more "primitive." The chief purveyors of this evidence were missionaries and colonial administrators who were not well trained in the art of observation. Failing to look deeply into the societies they reported on, they assumed that complex organization would resemble their own European societies and, failing to find it, concluded that other societies were less evolved, more primitive, and closer to original human nature. Their observations were then used by other disciplines and incorporated into social science theories of how societies developed and why humans behaved as they did.

THE PERSPECTIVE OF THE SCHOOL

Positivism itself is more accurately called a philosophy than a theory. Even as a philosophy, there are several varieties of positivism. Kaplan (1968:389) identifies two major forms of positivism. The first is a product of eighteenth-century Enlightenment philosophy with its emphasis on the importance of reason and experience. The second is a twentieth-century version known as "Logical Positivism" with a close association with mathematical reasoning and formal models of thought. Many today also associate positivism with various forms of statistical analysis. Within sociology alone, there have been several different understandings about the meaning of positivism (Halfpenny, 1982).

Many criminologists use the term positivism to mean an approach which studies human behavior through the use of the traditional scientific method. The focus is on **systematic observation** and the **accumulation of evidence** and **objective fact** within a **deductive framework** (moving from the general to the specific). Positivists, then, may study behavior from a biological or a psychological or a sociological perspective. The point is not the perspective from which the study is done, but the assumptions that underlie the methodology for doing the study.

Comte and the Methodology of Positivism

Much of the system of analysis which constitutes sociological positivism today was developed by Auguste Comte, a nineteenth-century French philosopher and social scientist who is credited with being the father of sociology. His approach to the study of social phenomena included an insistence on testable hypotheses, the use of comparative methods, the careful classification of societies, a systematic approach to the study of social history, and the study of abnormality as a means to understanding normality (Fletcher, 1975:ix-xi). Comte's work, among that of others, prompted scientific studies of human social behavior.

Early Nineteenth-Century Positivist Work

Perhaps the earliest of positivistically-oriented work on the subject of crime was that of two statisticians, Adolphe Quetelet of Belgium and Andre Guerry of France, in the 1820s and 1830s. Each examined the **social statistics** that were available in some European countries as if they were data from the physical sciences. Quetelet, for instance, applied probability theory to these data to produce a concept of the "average person," and then extended this concept to a study of crime rates. Among other things, he found variations in crime rates by climate and season, and observed the same age and sex differences as we find today among criminals (Quetelet, 1831).

Other early work was largely that of biologists and anatomists who studied the human body in hopes of establishing some relationship between it and human behavior. Some of this work distinctly predates any of the usual claims to the founding of criminology. A physiognomist of the sixteenth century, J. Baptiste della Porte, related characteristics of the body to criminality (Schafer, 1976:38). In the early nineteenth century, phrenologists measured and studied the shape of the head in an attempt to determine the relationship between brain and behavior. The chief practitioners of **phrenology**, Franz Joseph Gall and Johann Gaspar Spurzheim, believed that the characteristics of the brain were mirrored in bumps on the skull. They and their followers set about documenting the relationship between these bumps and behavior, especially abnormal behavior. The United States even had, for a short period in the 1830s, a journal devoted to the science of phrenology.

THE ITALIAN POSITIVISTS

The beginnings of criminological positivism are usually traced (although with questionable accuracy, as we have seen) to the work of three Italian thinkers, **Cesare Lombroso, Raffaele Garofalo**, and **Enrico Ferri.**

Lombroso, often called the father of modern criminology, was a surgeon who conducted systematic observations and measurements of soldiers, criminals, the insane, and the general population. The descriptive data painstakingly collected by Lombroso represented the use of an experimental method in "legal" medicine that was similar to criminal anthropology. Trying to account for mental and physical differences, he pointed out that criminals had multiple physical abnormalities that were of an **atavistic** (subhuman or primitive) or **degenerative** nature. These physical inferiorities characterized a biological throwback that Lombroso called the **born criminal.** He also reported that criminals manifested traits of sensory impairment, a lack of moral sense, particularly the absence of remorse, and the use of slang and tattoos.

In accord with the positivist tendency to categorize traits, Lombroso distinguished other types of criminals: the insane criminal, the epileptic criminal, and the occasional criminal, who for no biological reason but by the influence of circumstances or of surroundings was drawn to crime. This classification scheme was later modified by Enrico Ferri, one of Lombroso's students, to include the born criminal, those who committed crimes of passion, and the habitual criminal. According to Ferri, crime was caused by a number of factors including those that he called physical (race, geographics, temperature, and climate), those that he called anthropological (age, sex, organic and psychological) and such "social factors" as customs, religion, economics and population density.

Also building upon the work of Lombroso was Raffaele Garofalo who perhaps, most of all, was skeptical about biological explanations of criminal behavior. Garofalo believed that civilized people had certain basic sentiments about the values of human life and property; absence of these sentiments indicated a lack of concern for fellow humans. Finding a combination of environmental, circumstantial, and organic reasons for criminal behavior, he termed such behavior psychic or moral "anomaly," a deficiency of altruistic sensibility. He assumed that this psychic variation, which he carefully distinguished from insanity or mental illness, was more frequent among members of "certain inferior races" (Allen, 1973). Garofalo also commented on the legalistic nature of definitions of crime which limited them in application and situation. Instead, he formulated the more universal notion of **natural crime**, by which he referred to acts that all civilized societies would readily recognize as offensive.

Twentieth-Century Positivism

Following the work of the Italian Positivists, a good deal of effort was expended in the biological area. The family histories of criminals were examined and criminal **heredity** traced to certain ancestors (Dugdale, 1877; Goddard, 1913; Estabrook, 1916; Goring, 1913). Intelligence tests were developed and used to explain criminality through the concept of inherited **feeblemindedness** (Goddard, 1914; Burt, 1925). Other hereditary factors were considered through the examination of twins (Lange, 1930), general body types (Hooten, 1939; Sheldon, 1949; Glueck and Glueck, 1950), and even endocrinology (Schlapp and Smith, 1928). Work in this area continues today with research by Mednick and associates (1977) and the biosocial theorizing of Jeffery (1977).

Much of the literature on psychological influences on behavior has been the result of the ground-breaking work of Sigmund Freud. While Freud himself said little about crime, other psychiatrists have examined the effect of **unconscious conflict** on criminal behavior (Aichhorn, 1925; Abrahamsen, 1944; Friedlander, 1947). Perhaps the most notable work has been that of William Healy (1915; Alexander and Healy, 1935; and Bronner, 1936) in which he used the case-study approach to examine juveniles, and discovered that emotional trauma seemed to play a large role in giving rise to delinquent behavior. Other approaches have been the examination of **personality differences**, as with the MMPI (a complex personality test) and of psychopathic personalities (Hathaway and Monachesi, 1953), and recent work which suggests that there may be a "criminal personality" (Yochelson and Samenow, 1976).

On the sociological side, some early positivistic approaches encompassed both explanations of individual behavior and rates of behavior in society. The notion that behavior, including criminal acts, involved a process of **imitating** others was proposed by Tarde (1890). He theorized that there was short-term behavior (fashion) and long-term behavior (custom). People who were socially inferior would imitate those who were superior and copy their behavior. Thus, the use of a new and unusual technique for murder (as for instance the now-famous Tylenol poisonings) would spread. Tarde also suggested that, as population became more dense, behavior would be oriented more toward fashion than toward custom. On the statistical side, the ecological studies began by Guerry and Quetelet blossomed into a sociological criminology which set out to investigate the effect of social structure on crime. Since the 1920s, the American tradition of criminology has used the positivist technique of analyzing population data and crime rates, as well as using the systematic study of criminal behavior.

CLASSIFICATION OF THE SCHOOL

The Positive School is characterized by a *consensus* perspective. All the theories developed under its mantle assumed the existence of a core set of values in society which could be used to determine and treat deviance. From this point on, however, there are positivist theories which are both *structural and processual,* so that no definitive classification is possible. Sociological theories have, as a rule, been structurally oriented and *macrotheoretical,* while biological and psychological theories have been processual and *microtheoretical.*

SUMMARY

The work of the Positive School, diverse as it was, represented the first real concern with studying the behavior of the criminal. Embracing the scientific method, Positivists took a deterministic stance toward behavior and left behind the Classical School's insistence that humans are rational beings with free will. In the process, the notion of punishment for deterrence began to make less sense. If an individual's behavior were not predicated on rational decisions, then how could that individual be deterred? The thing to do, obviously, was to find those factors which caused the criminal behavior and remove (or treat) them. Further, it would be useful to be able to predict which individuals would be likely to become criminal and to treat them before they could harm themselves and society.

Positivists left behind the legal focus and concerns of the Classical School. In fact, for them the only reasonable definition of criminality was a social one. Legality simply got in the way of treatment because behavioral categories did not necessarily fit legal categories. If behaviors were socially undesirable, the individuals exhibiting them should be treated and returned to normalcy. Civil rights were of no concern if the real purpose of treatment was that of help. After all, how can one object to being helped; when a physician treats us, do we feel our civil rights have been violated? Thus early Positivists reasoned that criminals have no need to object when they are being treated by correctional experts.

Finally, positivism, as we have seen, is represented not only by biological theories of causality, but by psychological and sociological theories as well. In fact, most of the theories of criminology throughout the 1950s were positivistic in nature. As a general perspective, then, positivism has had an enormous effect on the way criminological theories have been constructed and the way that research has been conducted.

Major Points of the School

1. Humans live in a world in which cause and effect operate. Attributes of that world exhibit order and can be uncovered through systematic observation.

2. Social problems, such as crime, can be remedied by means of a systematic study of human behavior. Through the application of science, human existence is perfectible; or, at the least, the human condition can be made better.

3. Criminal behavior is a product of abnormalities. These abnormalities may be within the person, or they may exist as external social forces.

4. Abnormal features can be found through comparison with those which are normal.

5. Once abnormalities are found, it is the duty of criminology to assist in their correction. Abnormalities should be treated and and the criminal reformed.

6. Treatment is desirable both for the individual, so that he may return to normal, and for society, so that members of society are protected from harm.

7. The purpose of sanctions against criminals is, then, not to punish but to provide for treatment.

BIBLIOGRAPHY

ABRAHAMSEN, DAVID (1944). *Crime and the Human Mind.* New York: Columbia University Press.

AICHHORN, AUGUST (1925). *Wayward Youth.* New York: Viking (reprinted 1935).

ALEXANDER, FRANZ, and WILLIAM HEALY (1935).   *Roots of Crime.*
New York: Knopf.

ALLEN, FRANCIS A. (1972).   "Raffaele Garofalo," in Hermann
Mannheim (ed.), *Pioneers in Criminology,* 2nd ed.   Montclair,
NJ: Patterson Smith, 318–40.

BURT, CYRIL (1925). *The Young Delinquent.* New York: D. Appleton.

COMTE, AUGUSTE (1853).   *The Positive Philosophy of Auguste Comte,*
2 vols. Trans. Harriet Martineau. London: J. Chapman.

DRIVER, EDWIN A. (1972) "Charles Buckman Goring," in Hermann
Mannheim (ed.), *Pioneers in Criminology,* 2nd ed.   Montclair,
NJ: Patterson Smith, 429–42.

DUGDALE, RICHARD L. (1877).   *The Jukes: A Study in Crime,
Pauperism, Disease, and Heredity.* New York: Putnam's.

DURKHEIM, EMILE (1893).   *The Division of Labor in Society.* Trans.
George Simpson. New York: Macmillan (reprinted 1933).

ESTABROOK, ARTHUR (1916).   *The Jukes in 1915.* Washington, D.C.:
Carnegie Institute.

FERRI, ENRICO (1881).   *Criminal Sociology.* Trans. Joseph Killey and
John Lisle. Boston: Little, Brown (reprinted 1917).

FLETCHER, RONALD (1975).   "Introduction," in Kenneth Thompson,
Auguste Comte: The Foundation of Sociology.   New York:
Halsted, ix–xi.

FRIEDLANDER, KATE (1947). *The Psychoanalytic Approach to Juvenile
Delinquency.* London: Kegan Paul, Trench and Trubner.

GAROFALO, RAFFAELE (1885).   *Criminology.* Trans. Robert W. Millar.
Boston: Little, Brown (reprinted 1914).

GLUECK, SHELDON, and ELEANOR GLUECK (1950).   *Unraveling
Juvenile Delinquency.* New York: Commonwealth Fund.

GODDARD, HENRY H. (1914).   *Feeblemindedness, Its Causes and
Consequences.* New York: Macmillan.

_____, (1913).   *The Kallikak Family: A Study in the Heredity of
Feeblemindedness.* New York: Macmillan.

GORING, CHARLES B. (1913).   *The English Convict.*   London: H.M.
Stationery Office.

GUERRY, ANDRE M. (1833). *Essai Sur la Statistique Morale.* Paris.

HALFPENNY, PETER (1982).   *Positivism and Sociology: Explaining
Social Life.* Boston: Allen and Unwin.

HATHAWAY, STARKE, R., and ELIO D. MONACHESI (1953). *Analyzing
and Predicting Juvenile Delinquency with the MMPI.*
Minneapolis, MN: University of Minnesota Press.

HEALY, WILLIAM (1915). *The Individual Delinquent.* Boston: Little, Brown.

_____, and AUGUSTA BRONNER (1936). *New Light on Delinquency and Its Treatment.* New Haven, CT: Yale University Press.

HOOTON, EARNEST A. (1939). *The American Criminal: An Anthropological Study,* vol. I. Cambridge, MA: Harvard University Press.

JEFFERY, C. RAY (1977). *Crime Prevention Through Environmental Design,* rev. ed. Beverly Hills, CA: Sage.

KAPLAN, ABRAHAM (1968). "Positivism," in David L. Sills (ed.), *International Encyclopedia of the Social Sciences,* vol. 12. New York: Macmillan, 389–95.

LANGE, JOHANNES (1919). *Crime and Destiny.* Trans. Charlotte Haldane. New York: Charles Boni (reprinted 1930).

LOMBROSO, CESARE (1876). *L'Uomo Delinquente* (The Criminal Man). Milano: Hoepli.

_____, (1911). *Crime: Its Causes and Remedies.* Trans. Henry P. Horton. Boston: Little, Brown.

MEDNICK, SARNOFF A., and KARL O. CHRISTIANSEN (eds.) (1977). *Biosocial Bases of Criminal Behavior.* New York: Gardner.

QUETELET, ADOLPHE (1831). *Research on the Propensity for Crime at Different Ages.* Trans. Sawyer F. Sylvester. Cincinnati, OH: Anderson, (reprinted 1984).

ROTHMAN, DAVID (1971). *The Discovery of the Asylum: Social Order and Disorder in the New Republic.* Boston: Little, Brown.

SAVITZ, LEONARD D., (1972). "Introduction to the Reprint Edition," in Gina Lombroso-Ferrero, *Criminal Man: According to the Classification of Cesare Lombroso,* reprinted ed. Montclair, NJ: Patterson Smith, v–xx.

SCHAFER, STEPHEN (1976). *Introduction to Criminology.* Reston, VA: Reston.

SCHLAPP, MAX G., and EDWARD H. SMITH (1928). *The New Criminology.* New York: Boni and Liveright.

SELLIN, THORSTEN (1972). "Enrico Ferri," in Hermann Mannheim (ed.), *Pioneers in Criminology,* 2nd ed. Montclair, NJ: Patterson Smith, 361–84.

SHELDEN, WILLIAM H. (1949). *Varieties of Delinquent Youth: An Introduction to Constitutional Psychiatry.* New York: Harper and Row.

TARDE, GABRIEL (1890). *Penal Philosophy.* Trans. Rapelje Howell. Boston: Little, Brown (reprinted 1912).

WOLFGANG, MARVIN E. (1972).   "Cesare Lombroso," in Hermann Mannheim (ed.), *Pioneers in Criminology,* 2nd ed.   Montclair, NJ: Patterson Smith, 232–91.

YOCHELSON, SAMUEL, and STANTON E. SAMENOW (1976).   *The Criminal Personality,* vol. I. New York: Jason Aronson.

4

THE
CHICAGO
SCHOOL

INTRODUCTION

The University of Chicago established the first department of sociology in 1892 and through the mid-twentieth century was one of the dominant forces in American sociological thought. The diverse group of scholars who were associated with the department were collectively referred to as the "Chicago School" of sociology and criminology. Although we will focus on their work in criminology, many of the major themes that run through the studies are also found in the related fields of social psychology and urban sociology.

One recurrent theme was that human behavior was developed and changed by the social and physical environment of the person rather than simply by genetic structure. As David Matza (1969) wrote, it was assumed that people were complex creatures who were capable of great diversity in their lifestyles. In support of this view, the Chicago School considered the community to be a major influence on human behavior. They believed that a city was a natural human environment, "a microcosm of the human universe."

The methods by which the Chicago School studied the individual, and the city, were in themselves contributions to sociology and criminology. Developing an *empirical sociology,* researchers moved beyond social philosophy and armchair theory and began to study individuals in their social environment. At one and the same time, they examined people in the aggregate and as individuals. The *life history* provided a method of reaching deeply into the cumulative factors and events which shaped the lives of individuals. On the other hand, the *ecological study* technique allowed them to transcend individuality and, through the collection of social data, gain a sense of the characteristics of large groups of people. Combining the information gathered from individual cases with population statistics, the Chicago School was able to construct a framework which has been the basis for most of our criminological theories since then.

THE HERITAGE OF THE SCHOOL

The Social Heritage

Those who worked in the social sciences during the early twentieth century dealt with the development of the big cities, rapid industrialization, mass immigration, the effects of the First World War, Prohibition, the Great Depression, and more. Through it all, the members of the Chicago School looked to the city of Chicago itself as a source of questions and answers.

From a small settlement of the early 1800s, Chicago grew rapidly as "cheap labor" rushed to take advantage of canal work and inexpensive land. Opportunity attracted the abundant unskilled workers necessary to encourage industrial growth. Chicago doubled its population in the three decades between 1898 and 1930 as waves of immigrants transformed the simpler fabric of small-town uniformity into complex and conflicting patterns of urban life (Cressey, 1938:59). When the limits of industrialization were reached and the displacement of workers by technology began, the demand for a large, mobile, unskilled population disappeared, leaving a tangle of social problems ranging from inadequate housing and sanitation to homeless men, juvenile gangs, and vice.

Away from their closely-knit families and familiar communities, many people found that there was no one to whom they could turn in troubled times. Thousands of unemployed, male and female, young and old, became transients to avoid burdening relatives or friends. To counter these problems, many social work organizations and relief programs emerged between 1920 and 1930. Based on an implicit faith in the value of case work and rehabilitation, they aimed at employing and thus reforming the troubled masses. Though much attention was focused on the needs of the poor, it was also recognized that crime seemed to be fostered in the slums. The study of the slums, the immigrants living there, and crime became politically and socially relevant (Kobrin in Laub, 1983a:89).

As the last major wave of immigrants to the United States, southern and eastern Europeans received much of the blame for the nation's conditions. Among an existing population derived largely from western and northern Europe, the new immigrants were discriminated against and looked on as inferior stock. Aside from the prejudices inspired by peculiar customs and mannerisms, immigrants' loyalties were always suspect, particularly in times of war and political conflict. Children of immigrants, adapting more rapidly to the change in culture than did their parents and grandparents, were often embarrassed by their families and drew away from them, forming their own support groups and gangs (Whyte, 1943).

The melting pot of the American dream was also a law-enforcement nightmare as it became apparent that city neighborhoods had few purposes or customs in common at any one time. People often felt that the law was not theirs and refused to support or contribute to its enforcement. The search for a solution to these problems turned the city into a human laboratory for the new sociologists at the University of Chicago.

The Intellectual Heritage

Until the early twentieth century, American criminology had drawn from its European (Italian and English) heritage and supported popular Positivist explanations of crime, usually of the biological variety. Much of the previous research had linked feeblemindedness and hereditary factors with delinquency (Shaw and McKay, 1931:4). A change in this perspective came with the rise of cultural (rather than biological) theories of the behavior of individuals and groups.

As sociology moved into the study of crime, German influence began to take hold. As Bulmer (1984: 38) has noted in his history of the Chicago School, the leading figures in sociology had studied in Germany and were profoundly influenced by that experience. The German approach (and also that of the French sociologist Emile Durkheim), in contrast to the Italian Positivists, was pre-eminently social and cultural. At the same time, anthropology, under the leadership of Franz Boas and his students, had also dedicated itself to demonstrating that human nature was almost solely a product of culture, not of biology (Edgerton, 1976). Under this general social science umbrella, the foundation was being laid for a new sociological criminology.

In addition to the substance of their work, American sociologists were trying to establish a reputation for scientific analysis in their field, to counteract the image of sociology as philosophical and speculative (Short, 1971:xii). The scientific study of social problems, especially of crime, became one way for sociologists to enhance their academic and scientific credibility. Painstakingly, they gathered facts about urban life, watching and recording the growth and structure of the developing city.

CONTRIBUTIONS OF THE CHICAGO SCHOOL

Methodological Perspectives

Two major methods of study were employed by the Chicago School. The first was the use of **official data** (crime figures, census reports, housing and welfare records). This information was applied to geographical layouts of the city indicating areas of high crime, truancy and poverty. These charts and graphic portraits of social phenomena were maintained over periods of time and the figures displayed a stability that led to a revolutionary thought in crime causation, that certain areas of the city remained crime-prone even though various ethic populations came and went. The second method of study was the **life history**. W.I. Thomas first studied this form of folk psychology in Germany (Bulmer, 1983:36) and developed it into "ethnography" at the University of Chicago. This type of study shifted away from theoretical abstracts to the more intimate aspects of the real world. The life history or case study approach presented the social psychological process of becoming a criminal or delinquent. Sociologists became research explorers; they met, talked with, ate with, and virtually lived with their subjects. As the everyday lives of addicts, hobos and delinquents unfolded, the observers were invited to analyze the characters as they appeared in their natural environment, be it a slum, a street corner or a railroad car. Borrowing the idea of studying plants and animals in their natural habitat, researchers attempted to present a human ecology, to interpret people in time and space as they naturally appear. For this reason the Chicago School was often referred to as the Ecological School.

Ecological Theory

Perhaps as important as any other contribution of the Chicago School was the organic approach to the study of the community taken by Robert Park. Working under the assumption that the city was similar to a body with its different organs, Park sent his students out to examine the various organs, or "social worlds," of the metropolis (Farris, 1967:52). From these investigations and others, Park and Ernest Burgess produced a conception of the city as a series of distinctive concentric circles radiating from the central business district. The farther one moved away from the center of these **concentric zones**, the fewer social problems were found.

Using the ecological concepts from plant and animal ecology of dominance, invasion and succession, the general theory maintained that there were dominant uses of land within the zones. When those uses characteristic of an inner zone encroached on the adjacent outer zone, invasion occurred and that territory became less desirable. In time, the invading land uses would replace the existing land uses, resulting in a new social and physical environment. In this way, the inner zone would grow to include the adjacent outer zone, thus causing a ripple effect among all of the zones.

The first zone was the *central business district*, with its businesses and factories but few residences. The zone next to it was referred to as the *zone of transition* because it was the area upon which businesses and factories were encroaching. This area was not desirable as a location for residences and homes, but owing to its deterioration was the cheapest place to live. Immigrants, then, usually settled into this second zone because it was inexpensive and near the factories where they could find work. As they could afford to move, they moved into the third zone, the *zone of workingmen's homes*, and were themselves replaced in the zone of transition by another wave of immigrants. Other zones radiating out from there were increasingly more expensive to live in.

Subsequent research noted that social ills seemed to follow a pattern in which the most problems were found in the first zone and became progressively fewer in each succeeding zone. Shaw and McKay, for instance, documented that rates of delinquency, tuberculosis, and infant mortality followed the same decreasing pattern as one moved away from the central business district. The ethnographic and life history work of the Chicago School was then, in part, devoted to explaining the effect of these ecological areas on social life.

The observations made by researchers provided a picture of the city as a place where life was superficial, people were anonymous, relationships were transitory, and kinship and friendship bonds were weak. The Chicago School saw the weakening of primary social relationships as a process of social disorganization. In turn, **social disorganization** became the primary explanation for the emergence of crime. This was a particularly serious matter in the zone of transition because of the number of immigrants. Faced with the difficulty of maintaining primary relationships (and the difficulty of financially succeeding in a relatively class-bound society), immigrants retreated to the safety of their own native cultures. The relationship between immigrants and crime was finally seen, not as a product of heredity, but as a dual problem of social disorganization and of **conflict** with existing American culture.

Symbolic Interactionism

The social-psychological theory of **symbolic interaction** was one of the more lasting of the Chicago School theoretical perspectives. Although the Chicago School theorists who developed it never referred to it by this name (Blumer, 1969:1), symbolic interactionism developed from a belief that human behavior was the product of purely social symbols communicated between individuals. Perhaps the basic idea of symbolic interactionism is that the mind and the self are not innate but are products of the social environment. It is in the process of communicating, or symbolizing, that humans come to define both themselves and others. These symbols have meanings and they affect the way we see the world. If, for example, we are introduced to a juvenile delinquent, we may not see the person but may view him as "the standard juvenile delinquent," that is, we see someone who is all of the things we expect a juvenile delinquent to be.

Further, we pick up our own self-concept from our perception of what others think about us. These others are not necessarily specific individuals but, often, generalized types of people (Mead [1934] called this abstract person the "generalized other"). Thus, we create our own identities by reflection from others. W. I. Thomas' addition of situations led to understanding that we can have many identities, or self-concepts, depending on the setting in which we find ourselves. In the school setting, one may be a student; at home, a mother; at work, an insurance salesperson; at play, the team captain; in her parents' house, a child; and so forth. Each situation demands its own role, its own identity, its own behaviors. Moreover, in social life, one may incorrectly define the situation and behave inappropriately. To use Thomas' term, a proper **definition of the situation** is necessary in order for one to respond with acceptable behavior.

It was this recognition of the complexity and relativity of social life, with its multiplicity of required roles, that gave the Chicago School an understanding of deviance. This understanding required a concept that human behavior is *relative,* as are guidelines for that behavior. For the Chicago School, there were no absolutes, no set of universal rules which governed human behavior. First, there are places where normal behaviors would be defined by those outside of the place as deviant, in the "hobo jungles," for example. There people engage in "deviant" behavior by correctly defining the situation and following the roles expected of them The behavior is not, of course, deviant from the perspective of that specific setting but only from the perspective of outside society. Second, people can misdefine situations, act inappropriately, and become deviant. Here it is the misreading of the situational guidelines that leads to rule-violating behavior. For instance, in your home state you may legally make a right turn at a red light. Elsewhere, you may erroneously assume, much to your dismay when you get a ticket, that another state will allow the same practice.

Symbolic interactionism, then, provided a true social origin for both self-concepts and behaviors. It also gave us a relativistic (i.e., situational) understanding of the rules and guidelines that govern behavior. The Chicago School gave criminology an appreciation of the effect of social settings and situational values on crime and deviant behavior, which served to offset the universal-rule approach of the Positive School. The appearance of the labeling perspective in the criminological writing of the 1960s was directly related to this theoretical approach.

Culture Conflict

Having taken a relativistic position on human values and behavior, it was only natural for the Chicago School to recognize that conflict was common in society. Park had been impressed by the thoughts of one of the dominant German conflict sociologists, Georg Simmel, and incorporated the notion of conflict as a central component of an influential sociology textbook that he wrote with Burgess (1921). The common position was that conflict was a major social process, set in motion by the differences in values and cultures among groups of people. Louis Wirth, one of Park's students, wrote a thesis on cultural conflicts in immigrant families (1925) and later (1931) wrote about the relationship of the conflict of cultures to crime and delinquency. Another graduate (and faculty member) of the Chicago School, Edwin Sutherland also wrote (1929) on conflicting values and how criminal behavior arose from them.

The best statement of culture conflict theory, however, came from a scholar who was not a member of the Chicago School. Thorsten Sellin in his book *Culture Conflict and Crime* (1938) produced what is seen today as the seminal work on culture conflict. Although the book was to have been written with Edwin Sutherland, as a project of the Social Science Research Council, Sellin alone completed the work. The central thesis of culture conflict, though, was borrowed from the writings and teachings of Wirth and others at the University of Chicago (Sellin in Laub, 1983b).

Sellin's culture conflict theory revolves around the idea of **conduct norms**, or rules which govern behavior, which is very similar to W. I. Thomas' concept of definitions for behavior. Sellin wrote that one is reared with cultural values about proper conduct. The content of those norms vary from culture to culture; today we might also think of a subculture. Groups with social and political power can even use their conduct norms to control the definition of what crime is. Thus, the legal definition of crime is but the conduct norm for one particular social group. People come in conflict with these legal definitions of behavior accidentally or intentionally. If one's own culture approves an act, but the dominant culture does not, the stage is set for criminal behavior.

Sellin suggested that there are two main forms of culture conflict. The first, which he called **primary conflict**, occurs when there are two different cultures governing behavior, for example, when someone from one culture emigrates to another cultural area. The "old" culture can not simply be cast off, and for a while, will continue to influence the person's behavior. Sellin's classic example is that of the "Old World" family who moved to New Jersey. The daughter was seduced, and the father, following an "Old World" tradition, killed the young man to protect the family honor. He was arrested, yet could not understand why, since from his cultural perspective he had committed no crime. Another example of primary conflict is when one country conquers another and imposes its laws on the conquered people. For a while, citizens of the conquered nation will run afoul of some of the new laws simply because they are not used to them.

The other form of culture conflict is called **secondary conflict**. Here, Sellin was referring to smaller cultures, existing within a larger culture; the term we might use today is "subculture." People who live in a geographic area begin, over a period of time, to create their own set of values (conduct norms). While these values are not wholly different from those of the larger culture, there are enough differences to give rise to conflict. The people of an urban, center-city neighborhood, for example, may develop values leading to law-breaking. The agents of the law, of course, respond from the framework of laws based on middle-class values, laws which do not allow for subcultural differences. Thus, some subcultures see gambling and prostitution as legitimate behaviors, but the larger society has usually declared them illegal. Because of their values, then, the members of these subcultures are more likely to be arrested for gambling and prostitution than are other members of society whose values are more closely represented in law.

The notion of conflict, and culture conflict, as it grew from the Chicago School, strongly influenced American sociological criminology. Nettler, in his book *Explaining Crime* (1974:141), has stated that all subsequent social explanations have been based on the assumption that culture conflict is the fundamental source of crime. While this may be arguable, the relativistic, conflict approach of the Chicago School has been critical to the further development of criminology.

CLASSIFICATION OF THE SCHOOL

The Chicago School, as diverse in its viewpoints as it was, still shared a few commonalities. The main thrust of the work was, for instance, quite *positivistic* in character, albeit of a "newer" social variety. The assumption of determinism strongly characterized all of the work of the School, from the initial symbolic interactionism of Mead and Thomas to the statistical work of Shaw and McKay. Further, the positivistic emphasis on systematic observation and testing is clearly reflected in the work of the Chicago School.

It is difficult to classify the Chicago School as either structural or processual, largely because different members of the School stressed different factors in their explanations of society. Regardless of any assumptions they might have made about the structure of society (seen most clearly in the later work of Shaw and McKay [1942]), the dominant orientation was that of *process*. All of those associated with the Chicago School stressed the processes involved in behavior, the ways that people came to act in response to other people, real or imagined. Even the reliance on social disorganization (in reality a structural element) was derived from a different source from that of the anomie-strain theories which followed [see Chapter 6]. For the Chicago School the product of social disorganization was a variety of conduct norms and behavior rules, not societal strain. These various norms resulted in deviance as members of different groups or subcultures applied different definitions to the situations they commonly shared. Thus, the focus was on the process of gaining definitions and the underlying question was "How do individuals use their definitions of self and situation to produce behavior?"

Chicago School theorists were, at heart, *consensus* theorists. This does not mean that they did not emphasize conflict–they did. The assumption, however, was that consensus, or a natural conformity to cultural lifeways, was the initial pattern of human behavior. This is demonstrated by their appreciation of diversity in human behavior, yet it was a patterned diversity, one shared by the members of the culture to which one belonged. It was only where one group came into contact with another that conflict developed. And, of course, they recognized that society is made up of a variety of cultural groups; therefore, conflict is simply a fact of life.

Finally, the Chicago School produced chiefly *microtheories* (with the exception of culture conflict, which was a macrotheory). The social-psychological approach to the study of human behavior dominated almost all of the work of these people and became the common thread that wound through the diverse positions they espoused. There was more focus on the process of becoming deviant than there was on explaining how the structure of society affected deviant behavior. This fact is somewhat ironic, given that members of the Chicago School developed the study of ecological rates and prepared the evidence for most of the macrotheoretical work which followed.

SUMMARY

Although the sociological approach to studying modern problems started out as the interest of a small group of professors and students, the second generation of scholars expanded their interest into the realm of city programs and local research offices. The theoretical positions advanced by the Chicago School became the basis for much of the criminological work of the next three decades. The theoretical explanations that the members of the Chicago School (and their followers) gave to their research data still can be found behind many of the more "contemporary" criminological theories. In short, because of their widespread influence the Chicago School *was* the discipline of criminology itself until the late 1950s.

Major Points of the Theory

1. Humans are social creatures and their behavior is a product of their social environment.

2. Social environments provide cultural values and definitions that govern the behavior of those who live within them.

3. Urbanization and industrialization have created communities that have a variety of competing cultures, thus breaking down older and more cohesive patterns of values.

4. This break-down, or disorganization, of urban life has resulted in the basic institutions of the family, friendship groups and social groups becoming more impersonal.

5. As the values provided by these institutions become fragmented, several opposing definitions about proper behavior arise and come into conflict. Continued disorganization makes the potential for conflict even more likely.

6. Deviant or criminal behavior generally occurs when one behaves according to definitions that conflict with those of the dominant culture.

7. Social disorganization and social pathology are most prevalent in the center-city area, decreasing with distance from that area.

BIBLIOGRAPHY

ANDERSON, NELS (1923). *The Hobo.* Chicago: University of Chicago Press.

BLUMER, HERBERT (1969). *Symbolic Interactionism: Perspectives and Method.* Englewood Cliffs, NJ: Prentice-Hall.

BULMER, MARTIN (1984). *The Chicago School of Sociology.* Chicago: University of Chicago Press.

CHARON, JOEL M. (1979). *Symbolic Interactionism: An Introduction, an Interpretation, an Integration.* Englewood Cliffs, NJ: Prentice-Hall.

CRESSEY, PAUL F. (1938). "Population succession in Chicago: 1898–1930, *American Journal of Sociology* 44: 59–69.

EDGERTON, ROBERT (1976). *Deviance: A Cross-Cultural Perspective.* Menlo Park, CA: Cummings.

FARRIS, ROBERT E. L. (1970). *Chicago Sociology: 1920-1932.* Chicago: University of Chicago Press.

LAUB, JOHN (1983a). "Interview with Solomon Kobrin," in John Laub, *Criminology in the Making: An Oral History.* Boston: Northeastern University Press, 87–105.

_____ (1983b). "Interview with Thorsten Sellin," in John Laub, *Criminology in the Making: An Oral History.* Boston: Northeastern University Press, 166–181.

LEWIS, J. DAVID, and RICHARD L. SMITH (1980). *American Sociology and Pragmatism: Mead, Chicago Sociology, and Symbolic Interaction.* Chicago: University of Chicago Press.

MATZA, DAVID (1969). *Becoming Deviant.* Englewood Cliffs, NJ: Prentice-Hall.

MEAD, GEORGE H. (1934). *Mind, Self, and Society.* Charles W. Morris (ed.). Chicago: University of Chicago Press.

MCKENZIE, RODERICK D. (1924). "The ecological approach to the study of the human community," *American Journal of Sociology* 30: 287–301.

NETTLER, GWYNN (1974). *Explaining Crime.* New York: McGraw-Hill.

PARK, ROBERT E., and ERNEST BURGESS (1924). *Introduction to the Science of Sociology,* 2nd ed. Chicago: University of Chicago Press.

_____ (ed.) (1925). *The City.* Chicago: University of Chicago Press.

RAUSHENBUSH, WINIFRED (1979). *Robert E. Park: Biography of a Sociologist.* Durham, N.C.: Duke University Press.

REISS, ALBERT J., JR. (ed.) (1964). *Louis Wirth on Cities and Social Life.* Chicago: University of Chicago Press.

SELLIN, THORSTEN (1938). *Culture Conflict and Crime.* New York: Social Science Research Council.

SHAW, CLIFFORD R. (1930). *The Jackroller.* Chicago: University of Chicago Press.

_____, and HENRY D. MCKAY (1931). *Social Factors in Juvenile Delinquency.* Vol. II of *Report on the Causes of Crime.* National Commission on Law Observance and Enforcement, Report No. 13. Washington, D.C.: U.S. Government Printing Office.

_____ (1942). *Juvenile Delinquency in Urban Areas.* Chicago: University of Chicago Press.

SHORT, JAMES F., JR. (ed.) (1971). *The Social Fabric of the Metropolis: Contributions of the Chicago School of Urban Sociology.* Chicago: University of Chicago Press.

SNODGRASS, JON (1976). "Clifford R. Shaw and Henry D. McKay: Chicago criminologists," *British Journal of Criminology* 16: 1-19.

SUTHERLAND, EDWIN H. (1929). "Crime and the conflict process," *Journal of Juvenile Research* 13: 38-48.

THOMAS, WILLIAM I., and FLORIAN ZNANEICKI (1918). *The Polish Peasant in Europe and America.* Chicago: University of Chicago Press.

THRASHER, FREDERICK M. (1927). *The Gang.* Chicago: University of Chicago Press.

WHYTE, WILLIAM F. (1943). *Street Corner Society: The Social Structure of an Italian Slum.* Chicago: University of Chicago Press.

WIRTH, LOUIS (1925). *Culture Conflicts in the Immigrant Family.* Unpublished Masters thesis. Sociology Department, University of Chicago.

_____ (1931). "Culture conflict and misconduct," *Social Forces* 9: 484-92.

ZORBAUGH, FREDERICK (1929). *The Gold Coast and the Slum.* Chicago: University of Chicago Press.

5

DIFFERENTIAL ASSOCIATION THEORY

INTRODUCTION

Edwin H. Sutherland presented his theory of differential association in two versions, one in 1939 and the final version in 1947. The latter is still found in its original form in Sutherland and Cressey's *Criminology* (1978, now in its tenth edition). Sutherland created a general theory of criminal behavior by insisting that behavior was *learned* in a social environment. In fact, for Sutherland, all behavior was learned in much the same way. Therefore, the major difference between conforming and criminal behavior is in *what* was learned rather than in *how* it was learned.

In the 1920s and 1930s it was still common to assert that crime was the result of individual biological or mental defects. In the first two editions of his *Principles of Criminology*, Sutherland criticized and rejected both of these positions and, in doing so, advanced the cause of sociological criminology. Criminologist C. Ray Jeffery (1977:97) has even said that criminology is allied with the discipline of sociology today because of Sutherland. In a sense, his work set the tone for what we study and how we study it. Thus, we gain a great heritage from Sutherland and his theory may be the most popular criminological theory of this century.

THE HERITAGE OF THE THEORY

The Social Heritage

Many of the insights which shaped Sutherland's theory came from events of the 1920's and 1930's. The Federal Bureau of Investigation had begun to produce yearly reports of crimes known to the police, the Uniform Crime Reports, and evidence was growing that certain categories of people were more likely to be criminals than others. Since these people matched the Chicago School ecological data, official statistics seemed to support the view that crime was a part of the sociological domain rather than of the biological or psychological disciplines.

The Depression also served as fertile ground for sociological observations. Sutherland saw that people who previously had not been criminal, or even been in contact with criminals, committed criminal acts as a direct result of their impoverished situation during the Depression. Others, comparatively well off, took advantage of the economic situation and manipulated banks and stocks, all forms of "crime" in which Sutherland had an interest since the 1920s. Crime and other criminal behaviors were obviously not inborn, nor the results of feeblemindedness (a popular "intelligence" explanation of crime during the 1910's and 20's). Criminality was the product of situation, opportunity and, of course, values.

In addition, two other events occurred that may have affected Sutherland's views on criminal behavior: Prohibition and the criminalization of drug use. A colleague at the University of Indiana, Alfred Lindesmith, was working in both of these areas and had a great deal of interaction with Sutherland. These "new" forms of crime taught the astute observer that criminality was, in part, governed by the legal environment. Individuals who engaged in behavior which was not criminal at one point could become criminals by engaging in the same behavior subsequent to the mere passage of law. The focus on crime as defined by the legal codes was important to Sutherland, largely because he saw that society continually evaluated conduct in terms of adherence to the law. Though many Positivists of this time preferred expanded sociological (or non-legal) interpretations of crime, Sutherland saw the practical importance of working within legal parameters.

The Intellectual Heritage

The major intellectual influences on Sutherland's thinking came from the members of the Chicago School, particularly W. I. Thomas. The editor of a collection of Sutherland's papers even comments in his introduction that "Sutherland's theory of criminal behavior...may be regarded as an adaptation of the interactional sociology expounded by W. I. Thomas" (Schuessler, 1973:xi). In addition, symbolic interactionist materials developed by George Mead, Park and Burgess' conception of the city as a multifaceted organism, the ecological work of Shaw and McKay, and Sutherland's association with Thorsten Sellin were crucial to the actual development of his theory. Sutherland himself taught at the University of Chicago from 1930 to 1935 and, throughout his life, never went far from the Chicago area (Vold, 1951). The fact that Sutherland was born, raised and educated in a religious, rural Midwestern setting is also said to have influenced his perspective (Schuessler, 1973:x).

The two chief methodologies developed by the Chicago School, the examination of statistical information and the life history, were also important to Sutherland. Using the former approach, members of the Chicago School had already shown that, as the central area of a city was subjected to succeeding waves of immigrants, the high crime rates remained in the same *location.* Since the same high rates did not follow the residents who moved out into other areas of the city, it was obvious that something (values) was being transmitted that kept the crime rates high (Shaw and McKay, 1931).

In the search for the causes behind high crime rates in certain areas, several theorists proposed that the answer lay in the conflict between different cultural groups (Wirth, 1931; Sellin, 1938; Sutherland, 1929). Since the central city area was inhabited largely by immigrants (it was the cheapest place to live, and closest to the factories and businesses where they worked), it was suggested that their values and norms were simply different from those of the general population of Chicago. The source of the high crime rates, then, was not the area itself but the way in which the immigrants had been socialized to their native or "private" cultures in contrast to American or "public" culture (Schuessler, 1973:98).

The life history approach was also practiced by Sutherland in a series of interviews and contacts with a professional thief that began in about 1930. In a book based on this work, the thief, Chic Conwell, talked about learning the trade and the apprenticeship and recognition within the almost-institutionalized profession of thieves. This was, perhaps, for Sutherland the first analysis of how a group that associates itself differently, isolating and reinforcing its values, could grow out of the general culture.[1]

In formulating his theory, then, Sutherland drew upon three major theories from the Chicago School: ecological and cultural transmission theory, symbolic interactionism and culture conflict theory. In doing so, he was able to make sense of both the varying crime rates in society (the culture conflict approach) and the process by which individuals became criminal (the symbolic interactionist approach). Within this context Sutherland formulated a theory which was an attempt to explain both individual criminal behavior and the variation in group (societal) rates of crime. He had to take into account that criminal behavior was not necessarily different from conventional behavior, that values were important in determining behavior, and that certain locations and people were more crime-prone than others.

-----

[1]This was also the first appearance of the term "differential association." There is, however, some degree of controversy over the way the term was used in *The Professional Thief* and the theoretical usage which appeared later. Our own readings and the commentaries of others (Gibbons, 1979:50; Cressey, 1974:81; Snodgrass, 1973) suggest that the earlier use of differential association was much narrower than the concept Sutherland conveyed in his theory.

THE THEORETICAL PERSPECTIVE

The first suggestion of differential association theory came in the second edition of *Principles of Criminology* (1934). There, Sutherland (1934:51-52) stated:

> "First, any person can be trained to adopt and follow any pattern of behavior which he is able to execute. Second, failure to follow a prescribed pattern of behavior is due to the inconsistencies and lack of harmony in the influences which direct the individual. Third, the conflict of cultures is therefore the fundamental principle in the explanation of crime."

This statement became the basis for differential association theory which Sutherland developed.

The first version of the theory was proposed in 1939 with the publication of the third edition of *Principles*. This version referred to *systematic*[2] criminal behavior and focused equally on both cultural conflict and social disorganization and on differential association. He was later to eliminate the reference to systematic criminal behavior and limit the discussion of cultural conflict.

By the term "differential association," Sutherland meant that "the contents of the patterns presented in association" would differ from individual to individual (1939:5). Thus, he never meant that mere *association* with criminals would cause criminal behavior. Instead, the content of the communications from others was given primary focus. Crime was seen as a consequence of conflicting values, that is, the individual was following culturally approved behavior which was *disapproved* (and set in law) by the larger American society. Sutherland's own summary (1939:9) of the first version is that "Systematic criminal behavior is due immediately to differential association in a situation in which cultural conflicts exist, and ultimately to the social disorganization in that situation."

The second, and final, version of the theory was proposed in the fourth edition of *Principles* in 1947. There he expressly incorporated

---

[2]When Sutherland used the term "systematic," he meant either "criminal careers or organized criminal practices" (1939:4). It is the latter which causes the most problems of understanding. Based on the commentary in the 1939 edition of *Principles,* as well as on later sources (Sutherland, 1973:21-22; Cressey, 1960:3), the reference to "organized criminal practices" seems to have meant those behaviors with supporting definitions readily available in the community. This interpretation is supported by his choice of the term "adventitious" for non-systematic criminal behavior. The difference from the final version, where he dropped the term systematic, is not, perhaps, so marked as it would seem. Sutherland evidently felt that systematic criminal behavior included almost all criminal behavior (Cressey, 1960:3).

the notion that all behavior is learned and, unlike other theorists of the time, moved away from referring to the varied cultural perspectives as "social disorganization" and used the terms "differential social organization" or "differential group organization." This allowed him more clearly to apply the learning process to a broader range of American society. The final version of differential association was proposed in nine points:

1. Criminal behavior is learned.
2. Criminal behavior is learned in interaction with other persons in a process of communication.
3. The principal part of the learning of criminal behavior occurs within intimate personal groups.
4. When criminal behavior is learned, the learning includes (a) techniques of committing the crime, which are sometimes very complicated, sometimes very simple; (b) the specific direction of motives, drives, rationalizations, and attitudes.
5. The specific direction of motives and drives is learned from definitions of the legal codes as favorable or unfavorable.
6. A person becomes delinquent because of an excess of definitions favorable to violation of law over definitions unfavorable to violation of law.
7. Differential associations may vary in frequency, duration, priority, and intensity.
8. The process of learning criminal behavior by association with criminal and anti-criminal patterns involves all of the mechanisms that are involved in any other learning.
9. While criminal behavior is an expression of general needs and values, it is not explained by those general needs and values, since noncriminal behavior is an expression of the same needs and values. (Edwin H. Sutherland and Donald R. Cressey, *Criminology,* 10th ed. Philadelphia: J. B. Lippincott Co., 1978, pp. 80-82. With permission.)

Generally stated, then, the theory says that criminal behavior is learned in association with intimate others by interacting and communicating with those others. Two basic things are learned: the techniques for committing criminal behavior; and the definitions (values, motives, drives, rationalizations, attitudes) which support such behavior. It was stressed that a *relationship* must exist, that the transfer of skills or values cannot be accomplished by reading books or watching movies. The techniques may be thought of as the "hows," or the content of an act, and the definitions as the "whys," or the reasons for doing it.

Criminal behavior occurs, according to Sutherland, when there is an excess of definitions favoring criminal behavior, as opposed to those definitions which favor conventional behavior. The term "excess of definitions," however, does not mean a simple excess as we might think of in numbers, but instead, the *weight* of definitions as determined by the quality and intimacy of interaction with others (frequency, priority, duration, and intensity). Sutherland saw individuals as operating on a balance or ratio of potential good and bad behavioral definitions. One could become a shoplifter in the same manner as one becomes a bricklayer. Resulting behavior was often determined not only by the persons to whom one was exposed but also by the *absence* of alternative (criminal or non-criminal) patterns to fall back on.

In short, the theory of differential association does not necessarily emphasize *who* one's associates are; it focuses instead on the *definitions* provided by those associations. Indeed, it suggests that once the techniques of criminal behavior are learned, the values (definitions) supporting that criminal behavior may be learned from *anyone.*

The different social organizations to which we belong provide the associations from which a variety of forms of behavior, both favoring and opposing legal norms, can be learned. Thus, the term differential association implies that individuals as well as groups are exposed to differing associations with people who will vary in the importance they attach to respect for the law or law-abiding behavior. The individual, then, will lean toward or away from crime according to the cultural standards of his associates, especially those with whom he spends frequent and long periods of time (Schuessler, 1973).

CLASSIFICATION OF THE THEORY

Differential association is a *positivist* theory in that it focuses on the criminal and his behavior. For Sutherland, the real questions concerned criminal behavior, not how criminal law came to be, or even how the criminal justice system should be changed. Because of this approach, differential association is a *microtheory* when applied to etiological issues of criminal behavior.

In addition, the theory is oriented toward *conflict.* Sutherland's main objective was to explain how normative and cultural conflicts influence the learning of criminal behavior (Cressey, 1979). Sutherland's work focused on conflicting values, not on groups or classes with conflicting interests. In this sense, then, the theory is perhaps not as we might refer to contemporary conflict theories. The key to the classification of Sutherland's differential association as a conflict theory lies in his recognition that a large number of values or definitions exist in society, some of which are favorable to law-abiding behavior and some of which are not. This version of society does not suggest a consensus of values and Sutherland, in fact, referred to some laws as a product of the values of certain segments of society.

Finally, differential association is a theory of *process,* rather than of structure. Granted, it takes into account facts about the structure of society, and even argues for a structural explanation of crime rates, but the *focus* of the final version of the theory is on the process of becoming criminal. That is, Sutherland emphasizes the behavior itself and the processes which operate to create criminal behavior as opposed to conventional behavior. It is this area of the theory that has contributed to its classification by many criminologists as a symbolic interactionist theory.

SUMMARY

Sutherland's differential association theory remains one of the most popular of the theories of criminal behavior. Donald Cressey has carried on as a champion of the theory and as co-author of Sutherland's textbook. The theory itself is two-fold. First, it states that differential group organization explains varying crime rates and, second, that differential association explains individual criminal behavior. The former has been largely ignored since criminal behavior was the express focus of Sutherland's nine propositions.

Major Points of the Theory

1. Criminal behavior is learned in the same way as any other behavior.

2. Learning takes place in social settings and through what the people in those settings communicate.

3. The largest part of learning takes place in communication with those who are the most important to us.

4. The intimate social environment provides a setting for learning two things: the actual way to accomplish a behavior (if necessary) and the values or definitions concerning that behavior.

5. These values about certain behavior may be in opposition to the established legal codes. To the extent that we receive many statements about values, the *weight* of those statements (the importance and closeness of those who convey them) is more important than the actual number.

6. Criminal behavior takes place when the weight of the values concerning a particular behavior is in opposition to the legal codes.

7. The great number of groups and cultures in society make possible the learning of different types of values or definitions.

8. Some groups in society have more values in opposition to the legal codes than others (some are more in conflict); thus, some groups have higher crime rates than others.

BIBLIOGRAPHY

ADAMS, REED (1973). "Differential association and learning principles revisited," *Social Problems* 20: 458-70.

_____ (1974). "The adequacy of differential association theory," *Journal of Research in Crime and Delinquency* 11: 1-8.

AKERS, RONALD L. (1973). *Deviant Behavior: A Social Learning Approach*. Belmont, CA: Wadsworth.

_____ (1977). *Deviant Behavior: A Social Learning Approach,* 2nd ed. Belmont, CA: Wadsworth.

BURGESS, ROBERT L., and RONALD L. AKERS (1966.) "A differential association-reinforcement theory of criminal behavior," *Social Problems* 14: 128-47.

CHIRICOS, THEODORE G. (1967). "The concept of cause: a developmental analysis of the theory of differential association," *Issues in Criminology* 3: 91-99.

COHEN, ALBERT K., ALFRED LINDESMITH, and KARL SCHUESSLER (eds.) (1956). *The Sutherland Papers.* Terre Haute, IN: Indiana University Press.

CRESSEY, DONALD R. (1953). *Other People's Money.* New York: Free Press.

_____ (1954). "The differential association theory and compulsive crimes," *Journal of Criminal Law and Criminology* 45: 49-64.

_____ (1960). "Epidemiology and individual conduct: a case from criminology," *Pacific Sociological Review* 3: 47-58.

_____ (1960). "The theory of differential association: an introduction," *Social Problems* 8: 2-6.

_____ (1964). *Delinquency, Crime and Differential Association.* Hague, Netherlands: Martinus Nijhoff.

_____ (1966). "The language of set theory and differential association," *Journal of Research in Crime and Delinquency* 3: 22-26.

_____ (1979). "Fifty years of criminology," *Pacific Sociological Review* 22: 457–80.

DEFLEUR, MELVIN L., and RICHARD QUINNEY (1966). "A reformulation of Sutherland's differential association theory and a strategy for empirical verification," *Journal of Research in Crime and Delinquency* 3: 1–22.

GLASER, DANIEL (1956). "Criminality theories and behavioral images," *American Journal of Sociology* 61: 433–44.

_____ (1960). "Differential association and criminological prediction," *Social Problems* 8: 6-14.

_____ (1962). "The differential association theory of crime," in Arnold Rose (ed.), *Human Behavior and Social Process.*   Boston: Houghton   Mifflin, 425-42.

GLUECK, SHELDON (1956). "Theory and fact in criminology: a criticism of differential association," *British Journal of Delinquency* 7: 92-109.

GOLD, DAVID (1957). "On description of differential association," *American Sociological Review* 22: 448-50.

JEFFERY, C. RAY (1965). "Criminal behavior and learning theory," *Journal of Criminal Law, Criminology and Police Science* 54: 294-300.

_____ (1977). *Crime Prevention Through Environmental Design*, 2nd ed. Beverly Hills: Sage.

MCKAY, HENRY D. (1960). "Differential association and crime prevention: problems of utilization," *Social Problems* 8: 25-37.

SCHRAG, CLARENCE, and LEROY C. GOULD (1962). "Theory contruction and prediction in juvenile delinquency," *Proceedings of the American Statistical Association*, 1962: 68-73.

SCHUESSLER, KARL (ed.) (1973). *Edwin H. Sutherland: On Analyzing Crime.* Chicago: University of Chicago Press.

SELLIN, THORSTEN (1938). *Culture Conflict and Crime.* New York: Social Science Research Council, Bulletin 41.

SHAW, CLIFFORD R., and HENRY D. MCKAY (1931). *Social Factors in Juvenile Delinquency.* Vol. II of *Report on the Causes of Crime.* National Commission on Law Observance and Enforcement, Report No. 13. Washington, D.C.: U.S. Government Printing Office.

SNODGRASS, JON (1972). *The American Criminological Tradition: Portraits of the Men and Ideology in a Discipline.* Doctoral dissertation: University of Pennsylvania.

_____ (1973). "The criminologist and his criminal: the case of Edwin H. Sutherland and Broadway Jones," *Issues in Criminology* 8: 2-17.

SUTHERLAND, EDWIN H. (1929). "Crime and the conflict process," *Journal of Juvenile Research* 13: 38-48.

_____ (1937). *The Professional Thief: By A Professional Thief.* Chicago: University of Chicago Press.

_____ (1939). *Principles of Criminology,* 3rd ed.   Philadelphia: Lippincott.

_____ (1947). *Principles of Criminology,* 4th ed.   Philadelphia: Lippincott.

_____ (1949). *White Collar Crime.* New York: Dryden.

_____ (1956). "Development of the theory," in Albert K. Cohen et al. (eds.), *The Sutherland Papers.* Bloomington, IN: Indiana University Press, 13-29.

_____, and DONALD R. CRESSEY (1978). *Criminology,* 10th ed. Philadelphia: Lippincott.

VASOLI, ROBERT H., and DENNIS A. TERZOLA (1974). "Sutherland's professional thief," *Criminology* 12: 131-54.

VOLD, GEORGE B. (1951). "Edwin Hardin Sutherland: sociological criminologist," *American Sociological Review* 16: 3-9.

VOLKMAN, RITA, and DONALD R. CRESSEY (1963). "Differential association and the rehabilitation of drug addicts," *American Journal of Sociology* 69:129-42.

6

ANOMIE THEORY

INTRODUCTION

Anomie is a term closely associated with two theorists, Emile Durkheim and Robert K. Merton. When Durkheim introduced the term in his 1893 book, *The Division of Labor in Society,* he used it to describe a condition of "deregulation" occurring in society. By this, he meant that the general procedural rules of a society (the rules that say how people ought to behave toward each other) have broken down and that people do not know what to expect from each other. This deregulation, or normlessness, easily leads to deviant behavior. Durkheim used the term anomie later, in *Suicide* (1897), to refer also to a morally deregulated condition (see Olson, 1965) where people have inadequate moral controls over their behavior. Thus, a society may be anomic if people do not know when to quit striving for success, or how to treat other people along the way. Whichever of these two descriptions of anomie is used, a breakdown in either the rules of society or the moral norms, it is clear that Durkheim was talking about a disruption of normal societal conditions.

Anomie, then, refers to the breakdown of social norms and a condition where those norms no longer control the activity of societal members. Without clear rules to guide them, individuals cannot find their place in society and have difficulty adjusting to the changing conditions of life. This in turn leads to dissatisfaction, frustration, conflict, and deviance. Studying France and Europe after the Industrial Revolution, Durkheim saw economic crises, forced industrialization, and commercialization as factors producing anomie.

In 1938, Merton borrowed the concept of anomie to explain deviance in the United States. His concept, however, differed from that of Durkheim. Dividing social norms (or values) into two types, Merton talked of societal *goals* and the acceptable *means* for achieving those goals. In addition, anomie was redefined as a disjuncture (or split) between those goals and means as a result of the way society was structured, for example, with class distinctions. Deviance, then, could be explained as a symptom of a social structure within which "culturally defined aspirations and socially structured means" were separated from each other. Or, in other words, deviance is a product of anomie. It is Merton's treatment of anomie we will pursue in this chapter.

THE HERITAGE OF THE THEORY

The Social Heritage

Like the Industrial Revolution, the Great Depression of the 1930s also produced insights for sociologists. An entire generation of sociologists could observe the collapsing and deregulation of social traditions and the effect that it had upon both individuals and the institutions of society. As did Sutherland, Merton noted that crime was not necessarily an intrinsic part of the person and rejected individualistic views of pathology (Merton and Ashley-Montagu, 1940). The increasing popularity of Durkheim's discussion of anomie, when combined with the Depression, provided sociological insights into the connection between social structure and deviant behavior. Similarly, the notion of the division of labor opened up possibilities for an examination of the role of aspirations and opportunities in American society.

The importance of analyzing social structure itself became firmly grounded when the government's New Deal reform efforts focused on rearranging society. Sociologists and others found themselves moving away from the narrower applications of sociology and toward an examination of social structure as a whole (Merton, 1964:215). Given the popular belief of the time, that government was largely responsible for society's problems, Durkheim had provided social scientists with a ready-made explanation: Society was simply in a state of deregulation.

Another factor which affected criminology during the 1930s was the emergence of and emphasis on the collection of demographic data (information about people). Moreover, in examining both the ecological data collected by Shaw and McKay and the newly-created Uniform Crime Reports, it was evident that certain segments of society were burdened with high crime rates. These were the very same segments of society in which a relatively permanent state of deregulation could be observed. An obvious explanation was that, somehow, deregulation led to deviance. Finally, the idea that social class might be a crucial sociological factor in explaining social events was becoming popular. Just as sociologists were viewing other social behavior as being influenced by their social class position (Lynd and Lynd, 1929; Dollard, 1937), it occurred to theorists that an explanation of deviance based on social class differences might be productive.

The Intellectual Heritage

Merton was influenced by two sociologists during the 1930s. He was first introduced to the concept of anomie by the work of Pitirim Sorokin, whose 1928 book, *Contemporary Sociological Theories,* called attention to Durkheim's use of the term anomic suicide (Merton, 1964:215). Perhaps even more important, Merton had studied under Talcott Parsons whose approach to explaining social events emphasized the way society was structured. This approach became known as a "structural explanation."

Parsons saw society as the product of an equilibrium of forces (like a pendulum) which served to produce order. When the various components of the social structure became "unbalanced," that is, the pendulum swung too far to either side, society became disorganized. Durkheim's concept of anomie fit nicely into the Parsonian framework and was a major focus of Parsons' book, *The Structure of Social Action* (1937). With the translation into English of Durkheim's *Division of Labor in Society* in 1933, the use of social structure in explaining social behavior became accepted.

THE THEORETICAL PERSPECTIVE

Merton's anomie theory is, above all, a theory of deviance, that is, it does not focus on criminality. Further, Merton's conception of deviance is relatively general. When one conceives of a society which emphasizes well-structured **goals** for its members and equally structured avenues to reach those goals, deviance becomes any behavior that does not follow commonly-accepted values. For example, Merton uses the term deviance to refer to bureaucratic behavior, as well as to criminal behavior.

Merton noted that there are certain goals which are strongly emphasized throughout society (he uses the example of financial success). Society also emphasizes (legitimizes) certain **means** to reach those goals. When these goals are too strongly stressed, as Merton said financial success was in the United States, the stage is set for anomie. Not everyone has equal access to the achievement of legitimate financial success and, as a result, may search for other, perhaps illegitimate, ways of succeeding.

Because of social disorganization, the approved means to reach the success goals are not readily available to certain groups in society, even though the goals are said to apply equally to all. Certain groups of people, the lower social class and minorities, for instance, may be at a disadvantage in gaining business positions which would allow them to pursue the goal of financial success. When this inequality exists because of the way society itself is structured, Merton views the social structure as anomic. Given the evidence that there are several segments of society in which legitimate avenues to success are severely restricted without a corresponding reduction in the emphasis on achievement, U.S. society seems to be in a permanent state of anomie. The individuals caught in these anomic conditions (largely the lower classes) are then faced with the strain of being unable to reconcile their aspirations with their limited opportunities.

Of note, however, is the fact that legitimate means are not necessarily the most efficient methods of reaching the goals. Other means, although perhaps illegitimate or de-emphasized by society, may not only be available but also more efficient. It is also important to keep in mind that Merton was only using the focus on financial success as a consistent *example* throughout his work; he did not mean to imply that it was the only major goal which exists in American society. In fact, Merton later stated that:

> The theory holds that *any* extreme emphasis upon achievement—whether this be scientific productivity, accumulation of personal wealth or, by a small stretch of the imagination, the conquests of a Don Juan—will attenuate conformity to the institutional norms governing behavior designed to achieve the particular form of 'success,' especially among those who are socially disadvantaged in the competitive race. It is the conflict between cultural goals and the availability of using institutional means—whatever the character of the goals—which produces a strain toward anomie (1968:220).

The Modes of Adaptation

Merton presents five ways (modes) of adapting to this strain. If the emphasis on socially-approved goals and means is maintained even in the face of realization that the means are restricted, an individual will remain **conforming.** Most people follow this adaptation, Merton maintains; if they did not, the very existence of society would be threatened. The remaining four modes, however, represent a departure from this all-endorsing adaptation and thus are the "real" deviant modes of adaptation.

First is the case in which the emphasis on the approved goals of society is maintained while legitimate means are replaced by other, non-approved means. This mode of adaptation is called **innovation** and is the most common of the four deviant types. It is of interest that innovative means, especially for some segments of society, may actually be more *efficient* in reaching a goal than the approved means to do so. For example, instead of saving money and letting it slowly earn interest in a bank, a faster way of accumulating a lot of money would be to rob the bank.

If, on the other hand, the goals themselves are rejected and focus is shifted to the means, the mode of adaptation is that of **ritualism.** In this mode the means can become the aspirations of an individual, as when one may attempt to treat a job (means) as a form of security instead of using the job as a means of achieving success. In this example, keeping the job has become a goal by itself, resolving the frustration of unsuccessfully chasing the original goal.

A third mode, **retreatism,** involves a rejection of *both* the goals and means. Retreatists are those individuals who opt not to be innovative and, at the same time, need to resolve their inability to reach the important goals in life. Their solution is that they simply quit trying to get ahead. This pattern is best seen as "dropping out" of society and is exemplified by vagrants, drunkards and drug addicts.

The final mode of adaptation, **rebellion,** is of a different type from the other three. Where they emphasize rejection of means or goals, or both, rebellion focuses on the *substitution* of new goals and means for the existing ones. Merton's conception suggests that rebellion "leads men outside the environing social structure to envisage and seek to bring into being a new, that is to say a greatly modified, social structure. It presupposes alienation from reigning goals and standards" (Merton, 1968:209). These individuals, then, are precisely what the term indicates: rebels and revolutionaries.

In short, Merton's anomie theory explains how the social structure itself contributes to the creation of deviance on all levels, although the primary focus of the theory is on the lower class. Because of the societally-induced disjunction (separation) between cultural aspirations and the approved methods of attaining those aspirations, the lower class is most likely to exhibit deviant, non-approved, adaptive behavior.

CLASSIFICATION OF THE THEORY

Anomie theory is a *positivist* theory. In contrast to other positivist theories that locate pathology within the individual, anomie theory locates pathology within the social structure. Merton is explaining how a pathological social structure (one in which there is an undue emphasis on goals, especially economic ones, without corresponding avenues of access available to all the members of that society) serves to create a strain in certain segments of society and, ultimately, a push toward deviance. Because of this concern with structural strain, anomie theory is often referred to as a "strain theory."

The assumption of a *consensus* of values also characterizes anomie theory. American society imposes upon us the "right" things to do and the "right" ways to do them. Unless there is considerable unanimity about societal goals and means, there can be no anomic condition which results in adaptations to those goals and means. In other words, adaptations or deviations would merely be alternate modes of success or achievement.

Anomie is a *structural* theory. It focuses on the way society is structured and the way in which that structure serves to create deviance within American society. It does not, nor did Merton intend to, specify the process by which *individuals* become deviant. Instead, anomie deals with the pathology of existing social structure and the subsequent forms of deviance arising in the various segments of society as a whole. In short, Merton intends to explain variations in rates of deviance (Merton, 1968:186) among societal groups and not how the process of choosing among adaptations takes place. This broad scope and emphasis on explaining social structure also makes anomie a *macrotheory*.

Finally, and outside of our usual classification scheme, anomie theory is often called a *functionalist* theory. Functionalism presumes that it is desirable to explain a social phenomenon in terms of its effect on, and its consequences for, the social structure in which it exists. In other words, Merton uses the conception of cultural goals and norms to explain how they serve to produce both conformity *and* deviance within the social structure.

SUMMARY

Robert K. Merton's theory of anomie is among the most influential of all criminological theories, although presented as long ago as 1938. It continues to draw commentary and research, and several modifications have been offered (Richard Cloward's addition of an illegitimate opportunity structure is probably the most important; see the chapter on Subculture theories). Further, elements of anomie theory are, at least in part, found in more contemporary criminological theories (e.g., Hirschi, 1969:198).

The Major Points of the Theory

1. Most members of society share (or are socialized into) a common system of values.

2. This common value system teaches us both the things we should strive for (the cultural goals) and the most appropriate ways (societal means) to achieve those goals.

3. If the goals and the means to achieve them are not equally stressed, an anomic condition is created.

4. In a disorganized society, different degrees of access to these goals and means will exist. Thus the means will not be equally distributed within a disorganized society.

5. Some societies, such as that of the United States, may place too much stress on a particular success goal. This will, in a disorganized society, result in a striving toward that goal, but there will not be enough access to the means to achieve it.

6. Without reasonable access to the socially approved means, members of society will attempt to find some way to resolve the pressure to achieve. These alternative solutions are called "modes of adaptation."

7. The various modes of adaptation are formed by combinations of accepting, rejecting, or substituting for the goals and the means.

   a. If, in the face of moral pressure, the individual continues to "accept" the value of both the goals and the means, the form of behavior exhibited will be *conforming*. This is the most common form of adaptation.

   b. If the individual accepts the goals, but rejects the means to achieve them, the form of behavior will be deviant and *innovative*. Here, more available and faster ways of achieving the goals are created.

   c. If the individual sees the goals as unattainable (rejects them), but accepts the means anyway, the form of behavior will be deviant and *ritualistic*. In this case, the focus of the individual becomes the means then, rather than the ends.

   d. If the individual rejects both the goals and the means, the form of behavior will be deviant and *retreatist*. A person engaged in this behavior would no longer strive toward the goals and would not even continue in the normal stream of life.

   e. If both goals and means are rejected and then substituted for, the form of behavior will be deviant and *rebelling*. This form of deviance actually rejects the way society is currently set up and attempts to create a new form of society.

BIBLIOGRAPHY

CLINARD, MARSHALL B. (1964). *Anomie and Deviant Behavior.* New York: Free Press.

DOLLARD, JOHN (1937). *Caste and Class in a Southern Town.* New Haven, CT: Yale University Press.

DUBIN, ROBERT (1959). "Deviant behavior and social structure: continuities in social theory," *American Sociological Review* 24: 147-64.

DURKHEIM, EMILE (1893). *The Division of Labor in Society.* New York: Free Press (reprinted and translated 1933).

_____ (1897) *Suicide: A Study In Sociology.* New York: Free Press (reprinted and translated 1951).

HARARY, FRANK (1966). "Merton revisited: a new classification for deviant behavior," *American Sociological Review* 31: 693-97.

HIRSCHI, TRAVIS (1969). *Causes of Delinquency.* Berkeley: University of California Press.

LYND, ROBERT S., and HELEN MERRELL LYND (1929). *Middletown: A Study in American Culture.* New York: Harcourt, Brace and World.

MERTON, ROBERT K. (1938). "Social structure and anomie," *American Sociological Review* 3: 672-82.

_____ (1957). *Social Theory and Social Structure,* rev. ed. New York: Free Press.

_____ (1964). "Anomie, anomia, and social interactions: contexts of deviant behavior," in Marshall B. Clinard (ed.), *Anomie and Deviant Behavior.* New York: Free Press, 213-42.

_____ (1968). *Social Theory and Social Structure,* rev. and enlarged ed. New York: Free Press.

_____, and M. F. ASHLEY-MONTAGUE (1940). "Crime and the anthroologist," *American Anthropologist* 42: 384-408.

OLSEN, MARVIN (1965). "Durkheim's two concepts of anomie," *Sociological Quarterly* 6: 37-44.

PARSONS, TALCOTT (1937). *The Structure of Social Action.* New York: McGraw-Hill.

SOROKIN, PITIRIM A. (1928). *Contemporary Sociological Theories.* New York: Harper and Brothers.

7

SUBCULTURE THEORIES

INTRODUCTION

Criminological theories of the 1950s and early 1960s, with few exceptions, focused on juvenile delinquency. Many of the theorists set out to explain what they believed to be the most common form of delinquency: gangs. There was interest in explaining the origins of delinquent gangs and the context in which different types of gangs developed. At the same time, the cultures studied by the Chicago School began to be referred to by the new sociological term, "subcultures."

Combining these two topics, criminologists began studying gang delinquency and theorizing about delinquent subcultures. In separate works, Albert K. Cohen in 1955 and Richard A. Cloward and Lloyd E. Ohlin in 1960 combined the work of the Chicago School (and Sutherland) with Merton's anomie theory. Both focused on urban, lower-class, male, gang delinquency. Other theories included Miller's theory of lower-class "focal concerns" and Wolfgang and Ferracuti's theory of the subculture of violence.

Because of the differences among these theories, it is difficult to characterize them as a generic subculture theory. Therefore this chapter is divided into three sections. After a discussion of the heritage of the theories, we examine, in turn, Cohen's theory of the delinquent subculture, Cloward and Ohlin's differential opportunity theory, and two other theories, those of Miller and of Wolfgang and Ferracuti.

THE HERITAGE OF THE THEORIES

The Social Heritage

The period of the 1950s was a time of prosperity and a tremendous rise in consumerism. The values of the middle class had proven their superiority in a massive war effort and, consequently, for many it was difficult to conceive of anything other than the middle-class way as being "normal." It may even have been this same pride in "the American way" that helped to create the climate for communist-chasing during the McCarthy years.

Along with this spirit, the right to education was seen for the first time as something all Americans shared. As a result of educational benefits provided to military veterans, college enrollment climbed, and the middle class began to expect a college education for its children. Public schooling captured the attention of America and, by the end of the 1950s, the Soviet success in putting into orbit the first satellite resulted in a call in the United States for better education in the sciences. These events ultimately led to changes in the U.S. educational system.

At the same time, the peaking urbanization of the United States was producing increasingly deteriorated central city areas. Middle-class suburbs were developing, and the first housing subdivision was built outside Philadelphia. The Supreme Court outlawed segregation, but economic and territorial boundaries were already distinct. The problems of the cities were the problems of the people who lived there, principally the lower class. Delinquency was clearly a lower-class problem, and gangs were the most visible form of delinquency. With a clear "we-they" separation, middle-class America saw itself as superior to the lower class.

The Intellectual Heritage

The intellectual traditions behind theories of the 1950s were both the Chicago School theories and the Mertonian conception of anomie. Scholars associated with the Chicago School continued their study of crime and delinquency rates and researched the relationship between community and delinquency. Edwin Sutherland had become a dominant figure in criminology and spread the work of the Chicago School through several graduate students who came to study with him at the University of Indiana during the 1940s. These same students would themselves become prominent criminologists.

Robert Merton's theories had also become influential. His writings in sociology, and those of Talcott Parsons, had established a concern with social structure and the examination of social class differences. Within criminology, this "structural functionalist" approach captured the imagination of theorists who sought ways to reconcile Merton's structure with the Chicago School's process.

A final major influence on the subculture theorists of the 1950s was the writing of a researcher at the Chicago Area Project, Solomon Kobrin. He and others were examining street gangs and studying relationships between male generations in a lower-class community. They noted that there were ties between the political hierarchy and organized crime. These ties were so strong that Kobrin could refer to it as a "single controlling group" (Kobrin in Laub, 1983). From these observations, Kobrin (1951) introduced the concept of an integrated community. The degree of social control present in a community is, he wrote, dependent on how well the criminal element is organized and their relationships with conventional community leadership. When communities are organized and integrated, there is greater social control over the behavior of juveniles than is the case when integration is lacking. These insights turned out to be one of the keys to a future combination of the Mertonian and Chicago School paradigms.

COHEN'S SUBCULTURE OF DELINQUENCY

Albert K. Cohen's book, *Delinquent Boys* (1955), was the first attempt at solving the problem of how a delinquent subculture could begin. Cohen also attempted to integrate several theoretical perspectives, including the work of Shaw and McKay, Sutherland, and Merton. Although criticized severely (see especially Kitsuse and Dietrick, 1959; Bordua, 1960, 1961, 1962), his work was influential among criminologists.

After an examination of the research on juvenile delinquency, Cohen noted that delinquent behavior was most often found among lower-class males and that gang delinquency was the most common form. He also determined that gang subcultures were characterized by behavior that was **non-utilitarian, malicious,** and **negativistic.** In other words, Cohen saw in subcultural delinquency no rationale for stealing (other than seeking peer status), a delight in the discomfort of others, and an obvious attempt to flout middle-class values. Gangs were also characterized as engaged in various forms of delinquent acts (versatility), interested mainly in the present (short-run hedonism) as opposed to the future, and hostile to outsiders (group autonomy). These constitute the factors which had to be explained by a theory of the delinquent subculture.

Cohen declared that all children (indeed, all individuals) seek social **status.** However, not all children can compete equally for status. By virtue of their position in the social structure, lower-class children tend to lack both material and symbolic advantages. As long as they compete among themselves, the footing is relatively equal; it is in competition with middle-class children that lower-class children fall short.

The first major status problems confronted by lower-class children are in the school system. Not only do they have to compete with middle-class children, but they are evaluated by adults who use a "middle-class measuring rod," a set of standards which are difficult for the lower-class child to attain. In this competitive framework, the child loses ground in the search for status, among both fellow students and teachers. Those who feel the loss most will suffer **status-frustration.** Employing the Freudian mechanism of **reaction formation** (a defensive mechanism to overcome anxiety), Cohen speculated that a hostile over-reaction to middle-class values may occur.

Since many lower-class children are trapped in this status-frustration, various adaptations to the middle class take place. For some, adjustment to the "middle-class measuring rod" would result in a **collective solution** to the problem of status. This solution, Cohen suggested, also requires a change in the frame of reference under which status is attained. This is accomplished by jointly establishing "...new norms, new criteria of status which defines as meritorious the characteristics they *do* possess, the kinds of conduct of which they *are* capable" (1955:66, emphasis in original). Thus, a new cultural form, a **delinquent subculture**, is created to resolve problems of lower-class status.

It is this delinquent subculture that provides for the malicious, non-utilitarian, and negativistic character of gang delinquency. Abandoning and inverting the middle-class value system, the gang can achieve status simply by doing those things they do well. As long as the need for status exists, the delinquent subculture will exist as an available solution for lower-class, male youth.

It should also be noted that Cohen proposed, although in few words, theories of female delinquency and middle-class male delinquency. In both instances, he used the concepts of status-frustration and reaction-formation to explain the form of delinquent subculture available to each group. Females were seen as frustrated by the sexual "double-standard" and, through the reaction-formation process, resolve their status-frustration by engaging in sexually-oriented delinquent behavior. Middle-class males, on the other hand, become anxious about their "maleness" because of the child-rearing responsibilities of the mother. A reaction-formation results in a "masculine protest" against female authority and provides a middle-class male delinquent subculture. The subculture emphasizes behavior involving masculine activities, especially those revolving around the automobile, and thus leads to joy-riding, "drag racing," and being "bad."

Classification of the Theory

Cohen's subculture theory has usually been referred to as a *strain*, or *structural*, theory. While this is accurate, it is only partially so because, while the source of the subculture is strain, the theory focuses on the process by which the subculture is created. The latter part represents the influence of the Chicago School's process orientation. This duality also makes it difficult to classify the theory as either a macrotheory or a microtheory; instead, classification as a *bridging* theory is appropriate. In this respect, Cohen borrows from strain theory an explanation of social structure and proceeds to describe how delinquent subcultures come about. He does this from a *consensus* approach, meaning that society emphasizes reaching goals in the proper middle-class way. It is only after frustration develops from their inability to reach status goals that lower-class children find a need for alternative means. Similarly, the theory is clearly an example of sociological *positivism*. Cohen, in fact, tells us that there are certain forms of behavior to be explained (1955:21-48), and then develops the concept of subculture as a means of understanding those behaviors.

Major Points of the Theory

1. Members of society share a common value system that emphasizes certain values over others. In the United States, these values are closely associated with the middle class.

2. Most of these common values stress goals that result in the gaining of status; therefore, status becomes a generally approved goal in itself.

3. Opportunities to reach these goals are more often available to the middle class than to the lower class.

4. Societal institutions, especially the schools, reflect middle-class value-goals and use them to evaluate those who come in contact with the institution.

5. Lower-class youths, because of their limited opportunities, are often evaluated unfavorably by the school system, leading to frustration in their pursuit of status.

6. Unable to gain status through the use of conventional school opportunities (grades, social standing), lower-class youths rebel (reaction formation) against middle-class values while still keeping status as a goal.

7. Over a period of time, lower-class youths collectively create a new value system in opposition to middle-class values. The standards of this new value system are mostly anti-conventional and afford the youths opportunities for gaining status.

8. This "delinquent solution" is passed on through the transmission of values from youth to youth and generation to generation and fosters an ongoing delinquent subculture that provides

status for behavior which is "negativistic, malicious, and non-utilitarian."

CLOWARD AND OHLIN'S DIFFERENTIAL OPPORTUNITY THEORY

The theory which became known as "differential opportunity" theory had its origins as an article by Richard Cloward in 1959. Noting that Merton's anomie theory had specified only one opportunity structure, Cloward argued that there was a second opportunity structure. Not only was there a set of legitimate means to reach cultural goals, but there were standard illegitimate avenues as well (the **illegitimate opportunity structure**). This second source of opportunities became the background of the theory proposed in the book he wrote with Lloyd Ohlin, *Delinquency and Opportunity: A Theory of Delinquent Gangs.*

Cloward and Ohlin wrote that more than one way existed for juveniles to reach their aspirations. In those urban, lower-class areas where there were very few available legitimate opportunities, one could find opportunities of a different kind. Further, these opportunities were just as well-established and access was just as limited as were those in the legitimate structure. Thus, position in society dictated the ability to participate in both conventional and criminal avenues of success.

Using the writings of Solomon Kobrin (1951) on the concept of integrated conventional and criminal activity in lower class communities, Cloward and Ohlin stated that the form of delinquent subculture depended on the **degree of integration** present in the community. Actually, they suggested that without the presence of a stable criminal structure, lower-class juveniles would have no greater opportunity to succeed in life through criminal avenues than they would through conventional means. There would be no criminal "business" to join and to work one's way up through the ranks, no way to learn properly a criminal trade, and no way to become a "professional." Moreover, as people worked their way up though a criminal business, they could gain the wherewithal to enable them to slip over to legitimate business. In fact, this was exactly what Kobrin (1951:657) meant by community integration: Leaders in legitimate and illegitimate businesses shared the goal of profitability, membership in religious and social organizations, and participation in the political process.

Cloward and Ohlin proposed that there would be three ideal types of delinquent gang subcultures. First, where communities were fully integrated, gangs would act almost as an apprenticeship group for adult, organized criminal concerns. The primary focus would be on profit-making activities, and violence would be minimal. This subculture was called the **criminal subculture**. In these communities one could also find juveniles who would have access to neither of the opportunity structures. They would, over time, develop what Cloward and Ohlin called a **retreatist** subculture. Their primary focus would be on drugs and their gang-related activities would be designed to bring them the money for their drugs.

A non-integrated community would not only lack a well-organized and ongoing illegitimate structure but, according to Kobrin (1951:658), would also exercise very weak community control over the juveniles. Thus any gang subculture which would develop in one of these communities would exhibit unrestrained behavior. As in Cohen's delinquent subculture, the primary focus would be on gaining "respect." Violence, property damage, and unpredictable behavior would become the hallmarks of such gangs. Cloward and Ohlin called this form the **conflict subculture**. These gangs would cause trouble equally for the community's adult criminal element and for the conventional adults.

In sum, differential opportunity theory extends the anomie theory of Merton and adds the community-based observations of the Chicago School. Additionally, it suggests that subcultural patterns determine the form of delinquent behavior. For that matter, Cloward and Ohlin seem to suggest that the real problem of understanding deviance is that of explaining how different reactions (adaptations) to strain occur, and defining the context in which those reactions appear (Cullen, 1984: 39-49, 1986).

Classification of the Theory

Differential opportunity theory is usually termed a strain theory. But, as with Cohen's theory, it has elements of both *structure and process*. In combining the strain of anomie theory and the process of the Chicago School and differential association theory (Cloward and Ohlin, 1960:x), differential opportunity theory leans more toward structure. Yet, even while emphasizing the effect of one's place in the social structure, it attempts to explain the process by which the content of criminal lifestyles is transmitted. In a similar vein, this one is a *bridging* theory which leans slightly toward the macrotheoretical level. Finally the theory is both *positivistic* and *consensus*-oriented. It attempts to explain how behavior is developed and transmitted, and assumes, with Merton, a primary emphasis on reaching cultural goals.

Major Points of the Theory

1. Members of society share a common set of values which emphasize the desirability of certain life goals, especially that of success.

2. There are standard avenues for achieving these goals—legitimate and illegitimate.

3. These two general avenues (opportunity structures) are not equally available to all groups and classes of society.

4. Members of the middle- and upper-classes have primary access to the legitimate opportunity structure (business, politics), while members of the lower class have primary access to the illegitimate opportunity structure (organized crime).

5. In any urban, lower-class area, the degree of integration of these two opportunity structures determines the social organization of the community. The less the integration, the more the community is disorganized.

6. Communities with well-organized and integrated illegal opportunity structures provide learning environments for organized criminal behavior. In such communities, the male delinquent subculture takes on either of two ideal forms which are dependent on the degree of access to the illegitimate structure:

    a. When an opportunity to participate successfully in the illegitimate structure is available to young males, the subcultural gang type most commonly found will be a criminal gang. This form of gang serves as a training ground for the form of illegitimate activity found in the community.

    b. When opportunities for young males to join the illegitimate structure are as limited as are those to join the legitimate structure, the most common form of subcultural gang will be a retreatist gang. Here, the gang members are basically withdrawn from the community (they are "double failures") and the gang solves their problem of access to drugs.

7. Disorganized communities exert weak social controls and create disorganized gang subcultures. When young males are deprived of both legitimate and criminal opportunities, the common form

of gang subculture will be a conflict gang. Such gangs engage in violence and destructive acts against both opportunity structures.

OTHER SUBCULTURE THEORIES

Miller's Lower-Class Focal Concerns

After Cohen's work in 1955, Walter B. Miller examined lower class areas in Boston and came to different conclusions. As an anthropologist, Miller was familiar with ethnography, a research technique based on the direct observation of social groups in their own settings. Using this approach, he concluded that middle-class values were less important to gang delinquency than Cohen and others seemed to think. Thus Miller's theoretical perspective was more *conflict-oriented* than the consensus models of Cohen and of Cloward and Ohlin.

In a nutshell, Miller saw a society composed of groups (or cultures) which, while sharing some values, had otherwise differing lifestyles and norms. The lower class was simply a *separate culture* whose expectations and values were different from those of the middle class. Since the dominant culture was that of the middle class, the existence of different values was enough, in itself, to bring the lower class into conflict with middle-class values and those who enforce them.

Some portion of these lower-class values provided for proper male and female behavior and roles. Among other things, these values served to create male behavior which was delinquent by middle-class standards, but which was normal and useful to lower-class life. Miller suggested that it was these expectations that provided **focal concerns** (themes) for the male role by focusing on the importance of certain attributes. He characterized these desirable male attributes as emphasizing **trouble, toughness, smartness, excitement, fate,** and **autonomy**.

In examining lower-class life, Miller observed that a father-figure was commonly absent from the home and that the mother dominated the household. The dominance of this female role created a need for the young male to assert masculinity and practice the male role outside the home. The gang represented an opportunity to practice the male role and provided a sense of belonging and status.

From Miller's viewpoint, then, gang behavior is simply a reflection of appropriate lower-class male values. Miller summarized this by saying (1958:19) ". . . the dominant component of the motivation of 'delinquent' behavior engaged in by members of lower class [street] corner groups involves a positive effort to achieve states, conditions, or qualities valued within the actor's most significant cultural milieu." In short, the fact that gangs engage in delinquent behavior is directly attributable to a striving to maintain and exemplify the proper lower-class male role. It is simply normal, lower-class behavior which conflicts with the dominant culture.

Wolfgang and Ferracuti's Subculture of Violence

The last of the major subcultural theories was developed in 1967 by Marvin Wolfgang and Franco Ferracuti. Their work was substantively different from the other subculture theories, perhaps because it was developed almost a decade after delinquent-subculture theories and criminology had developed new concerns. Derived from Wolfgang's earlier study of homicide (1958), their subculture theory attempted to integrate a wide range of disciplinary approaches to understanding deviant behavior, amd they expressly state (1967:314) that the idea of a subculture of violence was a combination of theories (1967:314). From the sociological perspective they included culture conflict, differential association, and theories on culture, social, and personality systems. From psychology they chose theories on learning, conditioning, developmental socialization, and differential identification. Finally, they also incorporated findings from research on criminal homicide and other assaultive crimes.

Their theory may be summarized as follows: Though members of a subculture hold values different from those of the central society, it is important to realize that they are not totally different from or in total conflict with the greater society of which they are a part. Those in the subculture of violence learn a willingness to resort to violence, and share a favorable attitude toward the use of violence. This attitude, though possible to hold at any age, is most common in groups ranging from late adolescence to middle age. Persons who commit violent crimes, but are not identified by any link to a subculture, are distinctly more pathological and display more guilt and anxiety about their behavior than do members of the subculture.

SUMMARY

Along with anomie theory, the subculture theories dominated criminology during the 1950s and the early 1960s. Interestingly enough, the primary authors (Cohen, and Cloward and Ohlin) had training in both the Chicago School tradition and Merton's anomie approach. Thus, the main approach was that of reconciling these two "schools."

Even though they focused on gang delinquency, the concept of subculture was the real problem to be explained. For Cohen it was the question of how a subculture could develop; for Cloward and Ohlin, it was the attempt to explain the form that a subculture might take. In each case, they assumed that Merton was correct, that certain groups of people were disadvantaged in the great chase for success, and that the problem was to explain resulting deviant behavior.

Finally, subculture theories were important because they offered hope to a new generation of liberal-thinking people. The Kennedy and Johnson presidential administrations took the promise of restructuring society to heart and attempted to implement the major concepts of opportunity theory. They spent millions of dollars in the Great Society effort, most notably in Project Headstart and the Mobilization for Youth Project in New York City. Unfortunately, even this amount of money was not enough to successfully implement the theoretical concepts; restructuring society, even in small areas, proved to be too great a task.

BIBLIOGRAPHY

BORDUA, DAVID J. (1960). *Sociological Theories and Their Implications for Juvenile Delinquency.* Facts and Facets, No. 2. Washington, D.C.: U.S. Government Printing Office.

_____ (1961). "Delinquent subcultures: sociological interpretations of gang delinquency, "*Annals of the American Academy of Political and Social Science* 338: 119-36.

_____ (1962). "Some comments on theories of group delinquency," *Sociological Inquiry* 32: 245-60.

CLOWARD, RICHARD A. (1959). "Illegitimate means, anomie, and deviant behavior," *American Sociological Review* 24: 164-76.

_____, and LLOYD E. OHLIN (1960). *Delinquency and Opportunity: A Theory of Delinquent Gangs.* New York: Free Press.

COHEN, ALBERT K. (1955). *Delinquent Boys: The Culture of the Gang.* New York: Free Press.

_____ (1958). "Research on delinquent subcultures," *Journal of Social Issues* 14: 20-37.

_____ (1965). "The sociology of the deviant act: anomie theory and beyond," *American Sociological Review* 30: 5-14.

CULLEN, FRANCIS T. (1984). *Rethinking Crime and Deviance Theory: The Emergence of a Structuring Tradition.* Totowa, NJ: Rowman and Allanheld.

_____ (1986). "Were Cloward and Ohlin strain theorists? Delinquency and Opportunity revisited." Presented at the annual meeting of the American Society of Criminology, Atlanta, GA.

KITSUSE, JOHN I., and DAVID C. DIETRICK (1959). "Delinquent Boys: a critique," *American Sociological Review* 24: 208-15.

KOBRIN, SOLOMON (1951). "The conflict of values in delinquency areas," *American Sociological Review* 16: 653-61.

LAUB, JOHN (1983). "Interview with Solomon Kobrin," in John Laub, *Criminology in the Making: An Oral History.* Boston: Northeastern University, 87-105.

MILLER, WALTER B. (1958). "Lower-class culture as a generating milieu of gang delinquency," *Journal of Social Issues* 14: 5-19.

SCHRAG, CLARENCE C. (1962). "Delinquency and Opportunity: analysis of a theory," *Sociology and Social Research* 46: 167-75.

WOLFGANG, MARVIN E. (1958). *Patterns in Criminal Homicide.* Philadelphia: University of Pennsylvania Press.

_____, and FRANCO FERRACUTI (1967). *The Subculture of Violence: Towards an Integrated Theory in Criminology.* London: Tavistock.

8

LABELING
THEORY

INTRODUCTION

In the early 1960s a different approach to criminological theory was taken. Although it was an offshoot of older theories, labeling theory asked questions about crime and criminals from a new perspective, challenging previous definitions of deviance. Those associated with labeling argued that earlier theories had placed too great a reliance on the character of the deviant and neglected the variety of ways that people could *react* to deviance. This message was important enough that the position became known as the *societal reaction school.*

By de-emphasizing the criminal, labeling came close to the old Classical School in its concern for the action of official agencies and the making and application of laws. The theory also spurred interest in the way these agencies operated, so that for a while criminology was intensely interested in investigating the criminal justice process. Perhaps equally important, labeling sensitized criminology to the relativity of its subject matter and the middle-class values it had used to study criminals.

Some criminologists have debated the content of labeling theory, insisting that it is not a theory but instead a sensitizing perspective. This point has considerable merit, especially since those most important in the development of the position do not refer to themselves as labeling theorists; in fact, there would appear to be no identifiable labeling theorists. Further, since it is an offshoot of symbolic interactionism, labeling may not be new. Nonetheless, labeling has had a profound impact on criminology and on the study of deviance in general.

THE HERITAGE OF THE THEORY

The Social Heritage

At the end of the 1950s society was becoming conscious of racial inequality, segregation, and civil rights. The issue of underprivileged members of society became a real one. Civil rights protests and demonstrations were commonplace. Blacks protested their treatment in restaurants, theaters, buses, and in college admission. Education itself became the center of much of the civil rights movement. While equality did not come quickly, the white society grew more conscious of its treatment of minority groups.

Social changes of this magnitude were bound to influence social thinkers. Educators began examining ways to create classless schools. The Supreme Court handed down several important civil rights decisions. New programs began in the juvenile justice system with an avowed purpose of diverting juveniles before they were stigmatized with the label "delinquent." In short, the time was ripe for sociologists and criminologists to extend their theorizing about the effects of social class and minority status on those who came into contact with the criminal justice system.

The Intellectual Heritage

The intellectual heritage of labeling reflected the Chicago School's symbolic interactionism. The teaching and writing of both Mead and Thomas at the University of Chicago had influenced several creative people. Their students, some of whom returned to teach at Chicago, continued to spread the symbolic interactionist approach. A group of graduate students at Chicago during the late 1940s and early 1950s applied the approach to several areas of deviance. One of these students, Howard S. Becker, was to become the person most strongly identified with labeling.

In addition to the teaching of the Chicago School, their students and their writings introduced others to the concept of symbolic interactionism. One of the first contributors to labeling, Edwin Lemert, took a symbolic interactionist approach and applied it to social pathologies, including stuttering among West Coast Indians. Lemert taught this approach to his students, some of whom would become important advocates of the new societal reaction school.

The late 1950s also precipitated a methodological innovation in the measurement of deviance with the rise of self-report studies (questionnaires and interviews with juveniles who reported on their own delinquent behavior). Although earlier researchers had asked young people about their delinquent acts, it was the systematic work of James Short and F. Ivan Nye (1958) that began the comparison of admitted delinquent activity with official statistics. Their work suggested that official statistics such as Uniform Crime Reports and juvenile court records did not accurately portray those who commit delinquent acts. The differences in findings between self-report studies and official statistics suggested that the portrait of an "official" delinquent might be, in part, a result of the kind of person who came to the attention of the authorities. This implied that reaction by authorities rather than actual deviance might explain the disproportionate number of lower-class youths in the various delinquency statistics. The subsequent attempts to replicate the Short and Nye study also served to keep the topic current.

THE THEORETICAL PERSPECTIVE

Early Labeling Literature

Many criminologists trace labeling theory to Frank Tannenbaum's 1938 book, *Crime and the Community.* The "dramatization of evil," as Tannenbaum called it, suggested that deviant behavior was not so much a product of the deviant's lack of adjustment to society, but the fact that he or she had adjusted to a special group. Thus criminal behavior was a product of "...the conflict between a group and the community at large" (1938:8) where there were two opposing definitions of appropriate behavior. Tannenbaum wrote that a "tag" becomes attached when a child is caught in delinquent activity. The tag identifies the child as a delinquent, may change the child's self-image, and causes people to react to the tag, not the child. Thus, his argument was that the process of tagging criminals or delinquents actually helps to create delinquency and criminality (1938:19-20).

Definition of Crime

Labeling theory required a different orientation to deviance than that of previous theories. Noting that other definitions depend on statistical, pathological, or relativistic views of deviance, Becker pointed out that none of them does justice to the reality of deviance (1963:3-18). He saw that deviance can often be in the eye of the beholder because members of various groups have different conceptions of what is right and proper in certain situations.

Further, there must be a reaction to the act. That is, deviance must be discovered by some group which does not share in a belief in the appropriateness of the behavior, and it must subsequently be called deviance. To the extent that law reflects the values of that group, the behavior is labeled crime and the perpetrator a criminal. For labeling advocates, this distinction is important because it emphasizes that those who engage in criminal behavior are not synonymous with those who are labeled criminal. Thus the question of "Why do people become criminal?" becomes "How do people get reacted to as being deviant?" (Becker in Debro, 1970:167).

Studying the Reactors

Becker's interest in organizations and careers was in large part responsible for his defining deviance from outside the actor (those who are reacted to). The point he made was that, while sociologists ordinarily begin their study of other occupations by insisting that the entire organization be examined, the study of crime was focusing only on the criminal. The remainder of the "crime organization" (the social audience and the criminal justice system) was ignored in favor of an isolated criminal. Becker noted that he was merely following the occupational sociology approach: ". . . I approached deviance as the study of people whose occupation, one might say, was either crime or catching criminals" (Becker in Debro, 1970:166).

This concern of labeling gained impetus through the influential work of John Kitsuse and Aaron Cicourel (1963). They questioned the way criminologists used official statistics, especially the Uniform Crime Reports, in determining the amount of criminality in society. Their point was that official statistics may not represent levels of criminality as well as they reflect the behavior of those who take the reports of crime and compile the statistics. They suggested that official statistics were a better measure of who the police, and others, react to by arresting and initiating the criminal process.

Labeling as a Result of Societal Reaction

The labeling approach to deviance can be broken down into two parts: the problem of explaining how and why certain individuals get labeled, and the effect of the label on subsequent deviant behavior (Orcutt, 1973; Gove, 1975). The former view of labeling is really that of asking what causes the label; thus, the label is a dependent variable whose existence must be explained. The classic statement of this focus is Becker's:

> . . . *social groups create deviance by making the rules whose infraction constitutes deviance,* and by applying those rules to particular people and labeling them as outsiders. From this point of view, deviance is *not* a quality of the act the person commits, but rather a consequence of the application by others of rules and sanctions to an 'offender.' The deviant is one to whom that label has successfully been applied; deviant behavior is behavior that people so label (emphasis in original). [Howard S. Becker, *Outsiders: Studies in the Sociology of Deviance* (New York: The Free Press, 1963), p. 9. With permission of the publisher.]

By the *creation* of deviance, Becker meant that rules, circum-stances, characteristics of the individual, and reactions of those in the "audience" serve to separate those acts that are "deviant" from those that are not, even though they may appear as identical behaviors. It is not even necessary that the behavior exist; what is important is that the reactors believe in its existence. Thus it is the reaction to behavior that creates deviance. The problem is to explain how *outsiders,* as Becker referred to deviants, are chosen and labeled.

This approach to deviance meant that several facts about criminals needed explaining in a completely new way. Those who were arrested were, of course, predominantly lower-class, urban, young, and male. The new societal reaction school wanted to know why official agents reacted to these people more often than others. Their answers, exemplified by the earlier work of Garfinkel (1956), suggested that there were some common factors at work. The likelihood of reaction was greater if an individual were less socially powerful (age, social class), a member of a group with different values from the dominant group, or relatively isolated. Labeling theorists set about the process of determining how and why these types of people came to the attention of others.

Labeling as a Cause of Deviance

Labeling advocates were also concerned with the effect on the person who is labeled. This aspect of labeling treats the label as an independent variable, a causal agent, which then creates deviant behavior. There are two ways in which this may take place: (1) the label may catch the attention of the labeling audience, causing them to watch and continue the labeling of the individual; or (2) the label may be internalized by the individual and lead to an acceptance of a deviant self concept. Either of these processes may amplify the deviance (Wilkins, 1965) and create a *career* deviant.

Among the problems that a label creates is a subsequent reaction. Individuals who have been labeled become more visible in the sense that people are more aware of them. This awareness often causes them to be watched more closely and, thus, a second and third discovery of deviant behavior is even more likely than the first time. Especially important is that those who are in deviance-processing occupations (criminal justice agencies) closely watch individuals once they have come to the attention of their agency. In a sense, those labeled are the clientele of the criminal justice system and, like any other good business, the system keeps close tabs on its customers. It is difficult for the once-labeled, such as probationers, parolees, or ex-offenders, to escape the attention of this audience, and subsequent behavior is likely to be identified and re-labeled.

When the original label is more likely to be distributed among those with lower class characteristics, this attention effect serves to reinforce the image of those individuals as deviants. People who are identified as "deviants" then have fewer chances to make good in the conventional world. This means that conventional avenues to success are often cut off and illegal means may become the only way left open. Thus, labeling advocates argue that the lower class bears the brunt of the labeling process and is kept deviant through relabeling.

The second form of labeling effect is best reflected in what Lemert (1951) called **secondary deviance.** This concept suggests that, in addition to audience reaction, there is the possibility that an individual will react to the label. In this instance, Lemert assumes that the individual does not identify the initial act (primary deviance) as an important part of his or her self-image. People vary in their vulnerability, or sensitivity, to the reaction of others. If the original self-image is not strong enough, the labeled person may come to accept the image offered by others and change the self-image accordingly. The more often a person is labeled, the more likely it is that this change will take place.

Feedback is important to the process by which a new self-concept is internalized. Lemert describes the road to secondary deviance as follows (1951:77):

> . . . (1) primary deviation; (2) societal penalties; (3) further primary deviation; (4) stronger penalties and rejections; (5) further deviation, perhaps with hostilities and resentments beginning to focus upon those doing the penalizing; (6) crisis reached in the tolerance quotient, expressed in formal action by the community stigmatizing of the deviant; (7) strengthening of the deviant conduct as a reaction to the stigmatizing and penalties; (8) ultimate acceptance of deviant social status and efforts of adjustment on the basis of the associated role. [Edwin M. Lemert, *Social Pathology: A Systematic Approach to the Theory of Sociopathic Behavior* (New York: McGraw-Hill Book Co., Inc., 1951), p. 77. With permission of the publisher.]

In a sense, then, secondary deviance is gained through a trading back and forth until the labeled person finally accepts the label as a real identity. This often results in the person's joining a deviant subculture where further deviance is the product of the subcultural lifestyle. That is, future forms of deviant behavior are a product of the new role itself. Deviance in its secondary form is quite literally *created* by the labeling process.

Master Status and Retrospective Interpretation

Two other important labeling concepts are those of master status and retrospective interpretation. **Master status,** as developed by Hughes (1945) and Becker (1963), conveys the notion that there are central traits to people's identities which almost blind us to their other characteristics. These traits can be separated into those statuses that are almost always the prime characteristic (master status) of a person and those that are important but secondary (auxiliary status) traits. Examples of common master statuses are one's sex, jobs (as priest, as physician), and some forms of deviance (homosexuality). Where deviance is concerned, "criminal" is usually a master status. This makes it difficult for a person, once labeled a criminal, to be perceived as someone who may be trustworthy, even though the criminal act may have been an isolated one in the person's life.

Retrospective interpretation provides us with an idea of how identities can be reconstructed to fit a new label. Since the term "criminal" conveys a master status, it is difficult for people to understand how such a central fact about a person's character was not there before the criminal act and the labeling. In order to resolve this inconsistency, a process of reexamination takes place and past events and behavior are reinterpreted to fit the new identity. Thus, we think back to the past and see a criminal there all the time. Retrospective interpretation not only applies to people around the labeled person, but also to an official agency's reinterpretion of the person's records.

CLASSIFICATION OF THE THEORY

Because labeling can be viewed as both an effect and a cause (societal reaction and secondary deviance), there are two forms of labeling. Perhaps nowhere is the lack of a coherent "theory" more noticeable than in the attempt to classify labeling. Thus we will first provide a classification for the main thrust of labeling and then note any variation for other parts of the theory.

Labeling theory is predominantly a *processual* theory because of its concern with the way labeling takes place. It does, however, have some elements of structure in its discussion of the types of individuals most likely to be labeled. Similarly, labeling is largely a *classical* theory in its emphasis on crime, law, and processing rather than on criminal behavior. Lemert's version of secondary deviance, though, suggests a return to positivist concepts with his explanation of how the labeling process causes subsequent deviant behavior.

Other classifications are more straightforward. Labeling is clearly a variation of *conflict* assumptions, rather than being consensus-oriented. From its refusal to treat definitions of crime as universal, to its approach to explaining how reactions are distributed in society, the theory embodies cultural pluralism and value conflict. Finally, labeling is a *microtheory*. It focuses on the effect of societal reaction to the individual's behavior. Even where there is discussion of the way in which authorities react to deviance, the emphasis is on the process of labeling individuals instead of explaining how social structure creates labels.

SUMMARY

Labeling theory is a combination of several theoretical threads. With its heritage in symbolic interactionism and a divergent group of theorists, the core essence of labeling is hard to find. There are at least two main thrusts present. First, there is the concept of societal reaction. This component treats the problem of differences in reaction to deviance and focuses on the meaning of deviance to the audience. Second, there is the issue of secondary deviance, the problem of what a label means, and does, to the person labeled. Both of these thrusts are compatible yet they seem to suggest entirely different theoretical approaches.

The effect of labeling theory on criminology has been substantial. Perhaps most important, it caused criminologists to question the middle-class values they were using in their descriptions of deviance and criminality. Researchers began a critical examination of criminal justice agencies and the way in which those agencies processed individuals. The need to study deviant subjects *as part of humanity,* rather than as mere objects (Matza, 1969), also began to impress itself on criminologists. Even such criminal justice movements as diversion owed a direct debt to the work of those involved in the labeling movement. Finally, labeling was the precursor of conflict theories and, thus, in one fashion or another, occupied criminology for more than a decade.

Major Points of Theory

1. Society is characterized by multiple values with differing degrees of overlap.
2. The quality of any individual behavior is determined only by the application of values. The identification of a behavior as deviant occurs through a reaction to that behavior.
3. Deviance is a quality of the reaction and is not intrinsic to the behavior itself. If there is no reaction, there is no deviance.
4. Once behavior is perceived by a social audience, and labeled deviant, the individual who engaged in that behavior is also labeled as a deviant.
5. The process of reacting and labeling is more likely when those being labeled are less socially powerful than their audience.

Thus, deviance is more commonly ascribed to the less-powerful in society.

6. Reactors (individuals, social groups, law enforcement agencies) tend to observe more closely those whom they have identified as deviants and therefore they find even more deviance in those persons. Subsequent acts are reacted to more quickly and the label more firmly affixed.

7. The audience views an individual, once labeled, as being what the label says he or she is. A person labeled as a criminal is perceived to be first and foremost a criminal; other attributes that are not covered by the label may be ignored.

8. In addition to "becoming" a deviant for the audience, an individual may begin to accept the label as a self-identity. Acceptance of the label depends upon the strength of the individual's original self-concept and the force of the labeling process.

9. A change in self-concept will result in an internalization of the deviant character, with all of its attributes.

10. Further deviant behavior (secondary deviance) will be a product of living and acting within the role of the deviant label, often as a part of a deviant subculture.

BIBLIOGRAPHY

BECKER, HOWARD S. (1963). *Outsiders: Studies in the Sociology of Deviance.* New York: Free Press.

_____ (1973). "Labeling theory reconsidered," in Sheldon Messinger et al. (eds.), *The Aldine Crime and Justice Annual–1973.* Chicago: Aldine.

DEBRO, JULIUS (1970). "Dialogue with Howard S. Becker," *Issues in Criminology* 5: 159-79.

ERIKSON, KAI T. (1962). "Notes on the sociology of deviance," *Social Problems* 9: 307-14.

GARFINKEL, HAROLD (1956). "Conditions of successful degradation ceremonies," *American Journal of Sociology* 61: 420-24.

GOFFMAN, ERVING (1959). "The moral career of the mental patient," *Psychiatry: Journal for the Study of Interpersonal Processes* 22: 123-35.

GOVE, WALTER R. (ed.) (1975). *The Labeling of Deviance: Evaluating a Perspective.* New York: Halsted.

HUGHES, EVERETT C. (1945). "Dilemmas and contradictions of status," *American Journal of Sociology* 50: 353-59.

KITSUSE, JOHN (1962). "Societal reaction to deviance: problems of theory and method," *Social Problems* 9: 247-56.

_____, and AARON V. CICOUREL (1963). "A note on the use of official statistics," *Social Problems* 11: 131-39.

LEMERT, EDWIN M. (1951). *Social Pathology: A Systematic Approach to the Theory of Sociopathic Behavior.* New York: McGraw-Hill.

_____ (1967). *Human Deviance, Social Problems and Social Control.* Englewood Cliffs, NJ: Prentice-Hall.

LOFLAND, JOHN (1969). *Deviance and Identity.* Englewood Cliffs, NJ: Prentice-Hall.

MATZA, DAVID (1969). *Becoming Deviant.* Englewood Cliffs, NJ: Prentice-Hall.

ORCUTT, JAMES A. (1973). "Societal reaction and the response to deviation in small groups," *Social Forces* 52: 259-67.

SCHUR, EDWIN M. (1971). *Labeling Deviant Behavior: Its Sociological Implications.* New York: Harper and Row.

SHORT, JAMES F., JR., and F. IVAN NYE (1958). "Extent of unrecorded juvenile delinquency: tentative conclusions," *Journal of Criminal Law, Criminology, and Police Science* 49: 296-302.

TANNENBAUM, FRANK (1938). *Crime and the Community.* Boston: Ginn and Company.

WILKINS, LESLIE T. (1965). *Social Deviance: Social Policy, Action, and Research.* Englewood Cliffs, NJ: Prentice-Hall.

9

CONFLICT
THEORY

INTRODUCTION

Criminological conflict theories emerged on the heels of labeling theory. Similar in some ways to labeling, conflict theories focused on the political nature of crime and sought to examine the creation and application of criminal law. Although modern conflict theorist George Vold (1958) was writing at the same time as the early labeling theorists, his work attracted only mild interest. Perhaps because labeling was less politically oriented, and therefore more acceptable to conservative criminologists, it was more popular than conflict theories until the 1970s.

As was noted earlier, conflict theories share one fundamental assumption: that societies are more appropriately characterized by conflict rather than by consensus. This assumption allows for several varieties of conflict theory which can be viewed as if they were on a continuum. At one end, pluralist versions suggest that society is composed of a myriad of groups, often temporary, varying in size, all of which are struggling to see that their interests are maintained in any of a number of issues. At the other end, class-conflict versions argue that there are two classes present in a society, both of which are attempting to dominate that society.

Regardless of their position on this continuum of the number of groups and amount of power sought, conflict theorists view consensus as an aberration. That is, they see consensus as a temporary state of affairs that will either return to conflict, or will have to be maintained at great expense. It is the use of power to create and maintain an image of consensus, then, that represents the problem to be studied.

THE HERITAGE OF THE THEORY

The Social Heritage

The decade from 1965 to 1975 was a time of unrest in American society. After a period of optimism in the late 1950s and early 1960s, many people in the United States became disenchanted with their society. The success of the civil rights movement gave incentive to other "powerless" groups, such as women and homosexuals, who marched for recognition and for equality in social opportunities. Even students protested their treatment at the hands of college administrators.

The number of demonstrations against the Vietnam war grew in the years between 1965 and 1968. Though protest had been viewed as a political tool for students and blacks, it was soon adopted by others, including teachers, physicians, and members of the clergy. Despite its growing popularity as a means of expression, demonstration was still not seen as acceptable behavior; polls at the time showed that some 40 percent of the public believed that citizens had no right to even peacefully demonstrate (National Commission on the Causes and Prevention of Violence, 1969:23).

All of these events were part of a mood among younger people that questioned the middle-class values of America. The conventional lifestyles of their parents were often rejected as being hypocritical and morally corrupt. As Greenberg (1981:4) points out, even the criminal law was seen as a product of "...the relative power of groups determined to use the criminal law to advance their own special interests or to impose their moral preferences on others." People were discussing decriminalization of "victimless" crimes at the same time police were arresting civil rights workers. Finally, the political scandal of Watergate cast a shadow of doubt and cynicism on the morality and integrity of all aspects of American government.

The Intellectual Heritage

Conflict theories developed, in a sense, as an offshoot of labeling. While they had their own intellectual roots in a variety of German social theories (those of Hegel, Marx, Simmel, and Weber for example), it took labeling to prepare the way. Social scientists, reacting to the events of the time, began asking questions about social and legal structures that labeling had largely ignored. The early statements of both Richard Quinney (1965) and Austin Turk (1964), for example, were directed to the notion of societal reaction.

Even though conflict had not been popular, there was a smattering of conflict-oriented writing in sociology proper and even an early twentieth-century attempt to create a theory of criminality by combining Marxist and psychoanalytic approaches (Bonger, 1916). The most important impetus to conservative forms of conflict theory was the work of two sociologists, Lewis Coser (1956) and Ralf Dahrendorf (1958, 1959). It was their writings that spurred sociological interest in conflict and enlarged the perspective in the 1960s. Meanwhile, the rising radicalization of academia in general revived interest in the earlier work of Marx, and some scholars began to apply Marxist theory to crime and legal structures.

THE THEORETICAL PERSPECTIVE

There are many forms of conflict theory bound together only by the assumption that conflict is natural to society. Just as the theories of anomie, subculture, and differential opportunity could be grouped under consensus theory even though there are obvious differences among them, conflict "theory" contains at least as many different approaches. Here, however, they will be treated as one of two general forms: conservative or critical-radical. This would seem to be a common approach since others have made a similar distinction (Sykes, 1974; Gibbons, 1979; Farrell and Swigert, 1982; Vold and Bernard, 1986).

The Conservative Conflict Perspective

The central concept of conservative conflict theories is that of power and its use. These theories assume that conflict emerges between groups attempting to exercise control over particular situations or events. Thus the conflict approach is almost as if social issues were fields of combat with opposing armies fighting to see who will prevail and rule the land. As with armies, the matter of resources is a crucial one. It is the controlling of resources (money, land, political power) which provides the ability to successfully "fight" and to emerge victorious on a particular issue.

These social issues may arise out of problems of everyday life, because of lobbying by some group, or through the regular business and political process. In each, a decision will be made to take one course of action or another. Since several groups may have vested interests in the outcome of a decision, each will attempt to exert influence on their own behalf. Further, the amount of influence they will have is a product of the resources the group has available. Power to affect decisions is, therefore, synonymous with having resources.

If power can be equated with resources, then it seems evident that those who are higher up in the social class structure will be the more powerful members of society. Their influence in the making of social decisions, and their ability to impose values, will also be greater than those of the lower social classes. For conflict theorists, this explains the presence of a dominant middle-class value system in society. Similarly, the important statements of a society, its laws for example, are bound up in middle-class values.

Law itself represents a resource. If a group's values are embodied in law, they can use that law, and its enforcement, to their benefit. The agents of law, in their enforcement efforts, perpetuate the values embodied in law and thus help to keep in power those who already have power. Further, those who have values, or interests, that oppose the "winners" find themselves in the position of being the most likely targets of enforcement agents. At this point, labeling theory dovetails with conflict theory to produce an explanation of the reaction process by which the less-powerful come to the attention of law enforcement agents.

A final point is implied in the relationship between the use of power and the creation of law. Since law embodies the values of those who create it, law will also be more likely to criminalize the actions of those outside the power group. Put another way, people will rarely object to their own way of doing things; thus, any objections will be to the behavior of others. Why should a group expend resources to have their values upheld when the results will be detrimental to the group? Obviously, then, power not only helps a group to create law in its own interest, it also serves to reduce the chances that members of the group will be criminalized.

Two illustrative theories, characteristic of this form of conflict, are those of George Vold and Austin T. Turk. Vold (1958) produced a theory which emphasized the group nature of society and the various competing interests of those groups. He saw that "groups come into conflict with one another as the interests and purposes they serve tend to overlap, encroach on one another, and become competitive" (1986:272). Vold argued that groups had to be watchful of their interests and ever-ready to defend them. Thus, a group was engaged in a continuous struggle to maintain and improve its standing vis-à-vis other groups. From this viewpoint, Vold went on to discuss the presence of conflict in criminal law, writing that "...the whole process of lawmaking, lawbreaking, and law enforcement directly reflects deep-seated and fundamental conflicts between group interests and the more general struggles among groups for control of the police power of the state" (1986: 274). Finally, Vold observed that since minority groups lacked the ability to strongly influence the legislative process, their behavior would most often be legislated as criminal.

Austin Turk is another conflict theorist who saw social order as a product of powerful groups attempting to control society. This control is exerted by putting values into law and then by having the authorities enforce that law. Turk began his conflict work with an article in which he called for the study of criminality as opposed to criminal behavior (1964). Suggesting that the only explanation for criminality would be found in the criminal law, he proposed the examination of criminal law and its relationship to a definition of criminal status. His original concerns were to specify the conditions under which an individual would be defined as a criminal in an authority-subject relationship. He said that crime is a status which is given to norm resisters whose perception of social norms and reality is inadequate to anticipate the result of their actions (1966).

This concept of authority-subject relationships remains important in Turk's writings (1969, 1976). He sees as a fact of life that authorities must be dealt with, usually requiring a permanent adjustment of the subordinate to the powerful. There are, according to Turk, two major ways in which control can be exerted over a society. The first is coercion, or physical force. The more a population must be forced by the authorities to obey the law, the more difficult it will be to control that society. Thus, a delicate consensus-coercion balance has to be maintained by the powerful members of society.

The second form of control is much more subtle. This type is represented by the control of legal images and living time. The law itself can come to be seen as something that is more important than people. Further, there are two forms of law: the official list of undesirable forms of behavior and their associated punishments, and the established rules for processing people through the law-enforcement system. A legal process which is fashioned in favor of the powerful provides a degree of subtle control. Control of living time, on the other hand, is a concept recently developed by Turk (1976, 1982). He notes that after a period of coercion, a society will adjust itself to new rules. As time goes on, the generation of people who were part of the old society will die out. The remaining people have only experience with the new society, and thus are less likely to compare the new social order with the old one. When this happens, there will be little questioning of the rules of the new social order or, as Turk would put it, the relationship between authorities and the population (subjects).

These comments lead to a variety of propositions about criminality. Higher crime rates can be expected when physical coercion is more common than subtle forms of control. Similarly, the greater the power of the controlling groups, the higher will be the rate of criminalization for the less powerful. Finally, if the less powerful are organized, then there will be a greater likelihood of conflict with the authorities, with commensurately higher crime rates.

The Radical Conflict Perspective

Even more difficult than capturing conservative conflict positions with a broad stroke of the pen is a summary of radical conflict theorists. Their positions range from political anarchism (Tifft, 1979) through Marxism (Chambliss, 1975; Quinney, 1977; Spitzer, 1975) and economic materialism (Gordon, 1973) to value diversity (Pepinsky and Jesilow, 1985). It is even difficult to determine exactly what to call these different approaches (Bohm, 1982). Regardless of this variety, though, most of the current radical versions of conflict theory can be traced to the writings of Karl Marx (Greenberg, 1981).

While Marx said very little about crime and criminals, many radical criminologists have adapted his general model of society to their explanations of crime. Marx saw conflict in society as being due to a scarcity of resources and an historical inequality in the distribution of those resources, notably power. This inequality created a conflict of interest between those with and those without power. By the dawn of the Industrial Age, conflict had developed between two economic classes of society, the proletariat (the working class) and the dominant bourgeoisie (the non-working owners of wealth).

The main theme in this conflict of classes was that of control of the mode of production (the owning and controlling of productive private property). As the controlling class exploited the labor of the working class, a struggle developed. Since Marx felt that a group's position in society shaped its consciousness of that society, the working class was led to believe that the capitalistic structure of society was in their interest (a *false* consciousness). As members of the exploited class became aware of their true position and common interests, they would gradually join forces and initiate overt conflict against the dominant class. This conflict would take the form of a revolution which would overthrow the ruling class and allow a classless society to exist in a socialist world without economic exploitation.

Radical (Marxist) criminologists have assumed that the class struggle affects crime on three fronts. First, they have argued that the law itself is a tool of the ruling class. The definitions of crime found in the law are a reflection of the interests of the ruling class and serve to perpetuate existing concepts of property, which is the foundation of capitalism. At the same time, the behavior of the ruling class is generally *not* placed under the rule of criminal law (Michalowski and Bohlander, 1976) and instead, if placed under law at all, is found under administrative and regulatory laws. A belief in the validity of law deflects questions about its purpose and application, and results in members of the working class policing themselves. Radical criminologists would prefer to speak of law as a violation of more general human rights (Schwendinger and Schwendinger, 1970; Platt, 1974).

The second major position of radical criminologists is that they view *all* crime (in capitalist nations) as the product of a class struggle that produces individualism and competition. The emphasis on accumulation of wealth and property leads to conflict between classes and even within classes. Thus, the chase to get ahead "...manifests itself in the pursuit, criminal or otherwise, of property wealth and economic self-aggrandizement" (Bohm, 1982:570). Even violent crime is pictured as the result of the "brutal" conditions under which the working class must live (Quinney, 1977:53-54). For the working classes, then, it is their exclusion from the mode of production that creates a social structure conducive to criminal behavior.

Finally, Richard Quinney (1977) and Steven Spitzer (1975) have discussed the problem of surplus labor in capitalistic societies. Surplus labor guarantees that wages will be low, but too large a surplus of labor may cause problems. Spitzer lists five types of "problem populations" as (1) the poor stealing from the rich, (2) those who refuse to work, (3) those who retreat to drugs, (4) those who refuse schooling or do not believe in the benefits of family life, and (5) those who actively propose a non-capitalist society (1975). As long as the problem group is relatively quiet and poses no immediate threat to the ruling class, there is little need to expend scarce resources on their control. Skid row alcoholics are a typical group of this type, and Spitzer calls them "social junk." If, however, the group is active, then they pose a threat to the ruling class, and controlling them becomes important. These groups (political activists and revolutionaries) are called "social dynamite" and draw a disproportionate share of the control agents' resources.

CLASSIFICATION OF THE THEORY

First of all, conflict theories obviously assume that the society is *conflict-oriented*, rather than consensus-oriented. They also tend to focus on the political structure of society, especially the making and enforcement of law. Therefore, conflict theories represent a break with a positivistic tradition of explaining criminality and, instead, return to the concerns of the old Classical School. Conflict theories are more *classical* than positivist and emphasize crime rather than criminals.

Because of their emphasis on political and economic *structure*, conflict theories rarely engage in discussions of the process by which criminal behavior is produced. This leads to a classification of the conflict approach to crime as a *macrotheory*. Clearly, it is the nature of society itself, and its subsequent effect on social institutions, which is to be explained rather than behavior.

SUMMARY

The conflict perspective, whether conservative or radical, has changed the nature of criminological theorizing over the last two decades. Most criminologists will now acknowledge the presence of conflict in American society, although they reserve judgment about the extent to which it affects crime.

While it is difficult to characterize conflict theories because of their diversity (it is similar to discussing all consensus theories as if they were "a" theory), there are certain commonalities. First, of course, there is the assumption that conflict is natural to society. Second, resources are assumed to be scarce, or otherwise limited, and possession of these resources conveys power over others. Third, competition for resources always exists. Fourth, it is in this competition and use of power that law and law enforcement become tools to gain and maintain position in society. If a particular group gains control over enough resources and is able to maintain its position long enough, the conflict may result in a class system, with a ruling class and a subjugated class.

Major Points of the Theory

1. Conflict is a fact of life; society is most appropriately characterized by conflict.

2. Resources, both physical and social, are scarce and therefore in demand. It is the attempt to control these resources that generates the major portion of conflict in society.

3. Control of resources creates power and that power is used to maintain and expand the resource base of one group at the expense of others.

4. Once a group achieves dominance over others, it seeks to use available societal mechanisms for its benefit in order to assure that it remains dominant.

5. Law is a societal mechanism that provides the group in power with strong means of control over other, less powerful groups.

6. Laws are formulated to express the values and interests of the dominant group and to restrict behavior common to less powerful groups.

7. The application and enforcement of law leads to a focus on the behavior of less powerful groups, thus disproportionately "criminalizing" the members of those groups.

BIBLIOGRAPHY

BOHM, ROBERT M. (1982). "Radical criminology: an explication," *Criminology* 19: 565-89.

BONGER, WILLIAM A. (1916). *Criminality and Economic Conditions.* Trans. H. P. Horton. Boston: Little, Brown.

CHAMBLISS, WILLIAM B. (1975). "Toward a political economy of crime," *Theory and Society* 2: 152-53.

_____, and ROBERT B. SEIDMAN (1982). *Law, Order and Power,* 2nd ed. Reading, MA: Addison-Wesley.

COSER, LEWIS (1956). *The Functions of Social Conflict.* New York: Macmillan.

DAHRENDORF, RALF (1958). "Out of utopia: toward a reconstruction of sociological analysis," *American Journal of Sociology* 67: 115-27.

_____ (1959). *Class and Class Conflict in an Industrial Society.* London: Routledge & Kegan Paul.

FARRELL, RONALD A., and VICTORIA L. SWIGERT (1982). *Deviance and Social Control.* Glenview, IL: Scott Foresman.

GIBBONS, DON C. (1979). *The Criminological Enterprise: Theories and Perspectives.* Englewood Cliffs, NJ: Prentice-Hall.

GORDON, DAVID M. (1973). "Capitalism, class and crime in America," *Crime and Delinquency* 19: 163-86.

GREENBERG, DAVID F. (1981). *Crime and Capitalism.* Palo Alto, CA: Mayfield.

MICHALOWSKI, RAYMOND J., and EDWARD W. BOHLANDER (1976). "Repression and criminal justice in capitalist America," *Sociological Inquiry* 46: 95-106.

NATIONAL COMMISSION ON THE CAUSES AND PREVENTION OF VIOLENCE (1969). *The Politics of Protest: Task Force Report on Violent Aspects of Protest and Confrontation.* New York: Simon and Schuster.

PEPINSKY, HAROLD E., and PAUL JESILOW (1985). *Myths that Cause Crime,* 2nd ed., annotated. Cabin John, MD: Seven Locks Press.

PLATT, TONY. (1974). "Prospects for a radical criminology in the United States," *Crime and Social Justice* 1: 2-10.

QUINNEY, RICHARD (1965). "Is criminal behaviour deviant behaviour?", *British Journal of Criminology* 5: 132-42.

_____ (1970). *The Social Reality of Crime.* Boston: Little, Brown.

_____ (1977). *Class, State and Crime: On the Theory and Practice of Criminal Justice.* New York: McKay.

SCHWENDINGER, HERMAN, and JULIA SCHWENDINGER (1970). "Defenders of order or guardians of human rights?" *Issues in Criminology* 7: 72-81.

SPITZER, STEVEN (1975). "Towards a Marxian theory of deviance," *Social Problems* 22: 638-51.

SYKES, GRESHAM M. (1974). "Critical criminology," *Journal of Criminal Law and Criminology* 65: 206-13.

TAYLOR, IAN, PAUL WALTON, and JOCK YOUNG (1973). *The New Criminology: For a Social Theory of Deviance*. London: Routledge & Kegan Paul.

TIFFT, LARRY L. (1979). "The coming redefinitions of crime: an anarchist perspective," *Social Problems* 26: 392-402.

TURK, AUSTIN T. (1964). "Prospects for theories of criminal behavior," *Journal of Criminal Law, Criminology, and Police Science* 55: 454-61.

_____ (1966). "Conflict and criminality," *American Sociological Review* 31: 338-52.

_____ (1969). *Criminality and Legal Order*. Chicago: Rand McNally.

_____ (1976). "Law as a weapon in social conflict," *Social Problems* 23: 276-91.

_____ (1982). *Political Criminality: The Defiance and Defense of Authority*. Beverly Hills, CA: Sage.

VOLD, GEORGE B. (1958). *Theoretical Criminology*. New York: Oxford University Press.

_____, and THOMAS J. BERNARD (1986). *Theoretical Criminology*, 3rd ed. New York: Oxford University Press.

WILLIAMS, FRANK P., III (1980). "Conflict theory and differential processing: an analysis of the research literature," in J. A. Inciardi (ed.), *Radical Criminology: The Coming Crises*." Beverly Hills: Sage, 213-232.

10

SOCIAL
CONTROL
THEORY

INTRODUCTION

As the popularity of labeling theory began to wane and conflict theory moved toward more radical perspectives, control theory began to appeal to conservative criminologists. Although certainly not new, the term "control theory" refers to any perspective which discusses the control of human behavior (Empey, 1978). Such theories include explanations based on genetics, neurochemistry, sociobiology, personality, and environmental design among their various forms. *Social control theories* attribute crime and delinquency to the usual sociological variables (family structures, education, peer groups, for example), thus, their approach is different from other control theories.

Despite differences in the way social control theorists explain criminal behavior, they all share one basic thought. Rather than asking the normal criminological question, "What makes people criminal?", these theorists share a conviction that deviant behavior is to be expected. What must be explained, they say, is "Why people obey rules" (Hirschi, 1969:10). As a result some social control theories demonstrate a view of human nature which reflects the beliefs of Thomas Hobbes, a seventeenth-century English philosopher who was convinced that humans are basically evil. This view is not particularly crucial for the creation of social control theories, but these theories must at least assume a neutral human nature.

Another way to look at social control theory is to call it socialization theory. Since unsocialized humans, babies, for example, will simply act out their desires, it is the presence of other people which necessitates that those behaviors be controlled. The most important way we exercise that control is through the process of socialization. We teach the "right" way to do things (rules, norms) both informally, as in the family, and formally, as in school. In fact, much of our early upbringing is designed to socialize us so that we can function in society. Social control theories emphasize the quality of this process.

THE HERITAGE OF THE THEORY

The Social Heritage

Because of control theory's wide-ranging perspectives, and the fact that it spans a number of years, a discussion of the heritage of this approach has more to do with an explanation of its recent popularity rather than of its origins. Therefore, the discussion here will focus on explaining the theory's current acceptance.

While the 1960s brought about a questioning of social values and traditional institutions, there were also those who defended the status quo. Our previous characterizations of the decade should not be taken to mean that all, or even a majority, were protesting and voicing their opinions about change in America. Within any period, the dominant group is a relatively conservative one. Thus life for most people continued with relatively little change.

Some of the subtle changes taking place in society, however, would affect those who were more conservative. Religion became more important for many and the "born-again" movement grew throughout the 1970s. A cynicism about government fostered by Watergate further disillusioned those who had thought that the United States could become a "Great Society." Even the skyrocketing prices of gasoline, in the mid-1970s, heightened economic concerns. Finally, the taking of American hostages in Iran seemed to act as a catalyst for a politically conservative movement. As opposed to the liberal climate of the mid- to late 1960s, the mood of the next decade could be more accurately characterized as a growing conservatism.

The Intellectual Heritage

The intellectual heritage of social control theories is somewhat difficult to ascertain. It may, however, be accurate to say that the modern versions were originally developed as alternatives to strain theories. Clearly, this is the case for the 1950s theories of Albert Reiss (1951), Walter Reckless (1955), Gresham Sykes and David Matza (1957), and F. Ivan Nye (1958). For later theories, especially those of David Matza (1964) and Travis Hirschi (1969), the same may be inferred from their critical discussions of anomie and subculture theories. Even the usual identification of Emile Durkheim as the father of social control theory suggests that there is a connection with strain theories.

The rise in popularity of social control theory did not occur until the mid-1970s, suggesting that the blossoming of the theory may have been a result of three distinct trends within criminology. The first was a reaction to the labeling and conflict orientation and a return to the examination of criminal behavior. Conservative criminologists had little interest in the "new" criminology and wanted to return to the field's traditional subject matter, the criminal. Second, the rise of the study of criminal justice as a discipline helped to move criminology in a more pragmatic and system-oriented direction. The increase in the governments' interest and funding for criminal justice projects and crime fighting served to enhance the pragmatic nature of the movement. Criminology, as a result, was relatively free of theoretical work and left with its final theoretical inventions from the

1960s (Williams, 1984). The theory which met nearly everyone's personal explanation for criminal behavior was Hirschi's version of social control theory. Third, social control theories have been linked with a new research technique for locating delinquent behavior, the self-report survey (Vold and Bernard, 1986:247).

THE THEORETICAL PERSPECTIVE

Durkheim's Social Control Theory

Theories of social control all rely on social factors to explain how people are restrained from acting in ways harmful to others. The earliest explanation of this approach was that of Durkheim (1895). He said that a society will always have a certain number of deviants and that deviance is really a *normal* phenomenon. Further, deviance assists in maintaining social order, because there are vague moral "boundaries" that define which acts are allowed and which are disapproved. These boundaries specify the various degrees of disapproval for various acts, ranging from mild displeasure to legal sanctions and imprisonment. Since the actual boundary lines are not clear, it is the social reaction to someone else's deviant act that helps people determine what they should not do. Thus, Durkheim was saying that behavior is controlled by social reaction (displeasure, punishment).

Personality-Oriented Social Control Theories

In the 1950s several theorists presented social control explanations of delinquency. These theories set the stage for the contemporary approach to explaining crime and delinquency. Since Durkheim's time, the notion of social control had gone through several adaptations. The concepts of personality and socialization had become commonplace and one or the other was being used in most of the sociological work on deviance. In addition there had been several decades of research and writing on the ability of the family environment, religious institutions, schools, proper friends and associates, and community organizations to control delinquency.

Albert J. Reiss, Jr., (1951) combined concepts of personality and socialization with the work of the Chicago School and produced a social control theory which anticipated most of the later work. Although Reiss was using psychoanalytic theory and wrote at length on the importance of personality, his theory suggested that three components of social control explained delinquency (1951:196). He said that delinquency would result from any or all of (1) a lack of proper internal controls developed during childhood; (2) a breakdown of those internal controls; (3) an absence of, or conflict in, social rules provided by important social groups (the family, close others, the school). These three factors have been used, in whole or in part, by almost every social control theorist writing since then. In fact, Reiss' final statement may well represent the best summary of social control theory.

The next approach was developed by Walter Reckless, with subsequent work in collaboration with a colleague, Simon Dinitz. This theory, referred to as **containment theory,** explained delinquency as the interplay between two forms of control: internal (inner) and external (outer). Reckless said that a **self-concept** existed in people, formed when they were quite young. This self-concept provided either a "good" or a "bad" image of the self and acted as a buffer to outside influences. He also stressed that there were a variety of "pushes and pulls" toward deviant behavior that all individuals would experience. The effect of these inducements to commit delinquent acts depended upon the strength of an individual's inner and outer containments. If the self-concept were bad, outer social controls would have little effect on the individual and delinquency would be more likely to result. On the other hand, an individual with a good self-concept could withstand weak external social control and resist committing unlawful acts. While Reckless discussed both external and internal forms of containment, it was clear that he perceived the internal to be the more important of the two.

Social Bonding Theories

The concept of external social controls came into prominence with the work of David Matza. His first writings on the subject, co-authored with Gresham Sykes (1957), was a critique of Albert Cohen's subculture theory. In that critique, however, was the notion that everyone, even the lower class gang delinquent, is bound to the dominant value system of society. Sykes and Matza proposed that one becomes "free" for delinquent acts through the use of **techniques of neutralization.** These techniques allow individuals to neutralize and temporarily suspend their commitment to societal values, thus providing the freedom to commit delinquent acts. Sykes and Matza listed five forms of neutralization which they called *denial of responsibility, denial of injury, denial of the victim, condemnation of the condemners,* and *appeal to higher loyalties.* Further, they argued that these neutralizations are not just available to lower-class youth but are generally available throughout society.

Matza's later work (1964) included an explicit use of the term **bond to the moral order,** by which he meant the tie that exists between individuals and the dominant values of society. The problem for criminology was to explain how this bond could be either strengthened or weakened. Matza used neutralizations to explain how a person might be available for deviant behavior. Once neutralizations were used, he said, the individual was in a state of limbo or **drift** which made deviant acts permissible. From this point it was possible either to re-enter conformity or to commit a deviant act.

The thrust or impetus for action was centered around the *will* to do something. The will had two activating conditions: preparation, which provided for the repetition of old behavior, and desperation, which precipitated new behavior. These two theoretical components pulled an individual out of drift and allowed behavior to take place. Whether the behavior was conforming or deviant, however, depended on the situation and on the form of the neutralizations.

Other theorizing by Short and Strodtbeck (1965), while not directed to Matza's theory, emphasized the importance of **attachment** to peers and the rewards provided by those peers in strengthening or weakening bonds to society. Finally, Briar and Piliavin (1965), elaborating on an earlier work by Toby (1957) introduced the concept of **commitments to conformity.** By this they referred to the investment one makes in conventional images and appearances (student government president, for example). Those with the greater investments have correspondingly greater potential losses from being discovered to be a deviant. They meant not only material deprivation and punishment but also social deprivation. If one extends the idea of investments to material things, such as property, business, and wealth, then Briar and Piliavin can be viewed as a direct precursor to contemporary social control theory.

Hirschi's Social Control Theory

The most recent, and most popular, version of social control theory has been presented by Travis Hirschi (1969). Hirschi, synthesizing and elaborating on the work of other social control theorists, provided a clearer picture of what was meant by a social bond. Rather than seeing individuals as deviant or conforming, Hirschi, like Durkheim, believed that behavior reflected varying degrees of morality. He argued that the power of internalized norms, conscience, and the desire for approval motivated people toward conventional behavior.

As did Sykes and Matza, Hirschi saw that a person became "free" to engage in delinquency. However, instead of using neutralizing techniques, he blamed broken or weakened bonds to society.

Hirschi characterized the social bond as having four elements or dimensions (1969:16-34). The first, and most important, element is **attachment.** The strength of the attachments, or ties one has to significant others (parents, friends, role models) or to institutions (schools, clubs), can inhibit deviance. Second, **involvement** means the degree of activity, the time and energy, available for conventional or unconventional behavior. Those most occupied by conventional activities will simply have less time to be involved in deviance. **Commitment** represents the investment one has already built up in conventional society. This investment may take such forms as the amount of education, a good reputation, or the establishing of a business. Those with these forms of commitment to conventional society also have more to lose if they are caught engaging in deviant behavior. The last element, **belief,** constitutes the acknowledgment of society's rules as being fair. That is, one has a respect for those rules and norms and feels a moral obligation to obey them.

These four elements all affect the bond between an individual and society. Since all individuals exhibit some bonding to society, the question before criminologists is how much these bonds need to be weakened before deviance results. As any of the four elements are weakened, the freedom to engage in deviant behavior increases. What is less clear is the extent to which a weakening or absence of any one component of the bond will affect the other elements. For instance, does the strong presence of three of the elements, and the absence of the fourth, mean that deviance will result? They also, obviously, interact with each other to produce varying degrees of effect. While Hirschi did discuss some of the relationships among the elements, he saw this as an empirical question (an issue for research to answer) and preferred to keep the question open.

CLASSIFICATION OF THE THEORY

Social control theories are *positivist* theories in that they endeavor to explain behavior, albeit conforming behavior. Moreover, they imply (and in some cases overtly declare) that criminal behavior should be treated by increasing the influence of the family, schools, churches, and law-abiding peers. They also concentrate on the *process* by which the social bond is weakened, rather than on the structural reasons for the existence of that bond.

The issue of whether social control theories are consensus- or conflict-oriented is more difficult. They are based on the assumption that human nature is either neutral or, in the Hobbesian view, evil; therefore conflict seems inevitable. However, it is the assumption of the existence of a dominant moral order that orients social control theories toward a *consensus* view of society. Finally, these theories are in the *microtheoretical* range. Clearly, they focus on etiological issues rather than explaining social structure. In fact, other than assuming that a moral order exists, they state little about social structure itself. Instead, they set forth at length how the weakening of the effect of various social institutions allows for an increase in deviant behavior among individuals.

SUMMARY

Social control theory, for all its recent popularity, is not new. Moreover, it is probably the one theoretical approach most closely matching the public's conception of why people become criminals. Whether one believes that a person becomes criminal because of associating with the wrong friends, because of an improper family upbringing, because of a lack of religion, or because of a lack of education, social control theory can be seen to reflect that belief. Further, for criminologists themselves, this theory contains bits and pieces of the theories of social disorganization, differential association, and anomie, making it especially attractive to those criminologists who have been reluctant to embrace conflict theories.

In sum, social control theory takes a view of human nature which assumes that deviance is natural (which makes it similar to labeling in this regard). Conformity, then, is the real question worthy of explanation. Positing a moral order, or a conventional framework in society, social control theory finds common social institutions that strengthen that bond. When these institutions are weakened, whatever the cause, the bond that ties individuals to the moral order is also weakened. This weakened bond automatically permits a greater degree of deviance to occur.

Major Points of the Theory

1. Self preservation and gratification are characteristic of human nature; therefore human behavior tends to be "self-interested".

2. Human behavior must be restrained and regulated for the benefit of all.

3. The rules and regulations for living in a society constitute a moral order.

4. Humans are bound to the moral order beginning with childhood socialization and later through the institutions of society.

5. The bond to the moral order is composed of elements that maintain and strengthen conformity.

6. The elements of the bond include attachment to important others and institutions, commitment to or investment in conventional society, involvement in conventional activities, and belief in societal values.

7. These elements are present in varying degrees. To the extent that they may become weak, or are absent, individuals have more freedom to pursue self-interested and deviant behavior.

BIBLIOGRAPHY

BRIAR, SCOTT and IRVING PILIAVIN (1965). "Delinquency, situational inducements, and commitment to conformity," *Social Problems* 13: 33–45.

CONGER, RAND (1976). "Social control and social learning models of delinquent behavior: a synthesis," *Criminology* 17: 17–40.

DURKHEIM, EMILE (1895). *The Rules of the Sociological Method.* Trans. Sarah A. Solovay and John H. Mueller. New York: Free Press (reprinted 1965).

ELLIOT, DELBERT S., DAVID HUIZINGA, and SUZANNE S. AGETON (1985). *Explaining Delinquency and Drug Use.* Beverly Hills: Sage.

EMPEY, LAMAR T. (1978). *American Delinquency: Its Meaning and Construction.* Homewood, IL: Dorsey.

HIRSCHI, TRAVIS (1969). *Causes of Delinquency.* Berkeley: University of California Press.

MATZA, DAVID (1964). *Delinquency and Drift.* New York: John Wiley.

NYE, F. IVAN (1958). *Family Relationships and Delinquent Behavior.* New York: John Wiley.

RECKLESS, WALTER C. (1955). *The Crime Problem.* New York: Appleton-Century-Crofts.

_____ and SIMON DINITZ (1967). "Pioneering with self-concept as a vulnerability factor in delinquency," *Journal of Criminal Law, Criminology, and Police Science* 58: 515–23.

_____, SIMON DINITZ, and ELLEN MURRAY (1956). "Self-concept as an insulator against delinquency," *American Sociological Review* 21: 744-56.

REISS, ALBERT J., JR. (1951). "Delinquency as the failure of personal and social controls," *American Sociological Review* 16: 196-207.

SHORT, JAMES F., JR., and FRED L. STRODTBECK (1965). *Group Process and Gang Delinquency.* Chicago: University of Chicago Press.

SYKES, GRESHAM M., and DAVID MATZA (1957). "Techniques of neutralization: a theory of delinquency," *American Sociological Review* 22: 664-70.

TOBY, JACKSON (1957). "Social disorganization and stake in conformity: complementary factors in the predatory behavior of hoodlums," *Journal of Criminal Law, Criminology, and Police Science* 48: 12-17.

VOLD, GEORGE B., and THOMAS J. BERNARD (1986). *Theoretical Criminology,* 3rd ed. New York: Oxford University Press.

WILLIAMS, FRANK P., III (1984). "The demise of the criminological imagination: a critique of recent criminology," *Justice Quarterly* 1: 91-106.

11

SOCIAL
LEARNING
THEORY

INTRODUCTION

Even though social learning theory was developed a short time before Hirschi's social control theory (1965-6), it is newer than the other versions of social control theory and has become popular only in the last ten years or so. There are really two theories under this generic name. The first was developed by C. Ray Jeffery as a direct application of popular learning theories from psychology. The other, which has received greater acceptance by criminologists, is Ronald Akers' *social* learning theory.

Both these theories rely on behavioral psychology. There are two general types of psychological approaches: Skinnerian, or operant theory, and social learning theory. B. F. Skinner's original version of operant theory allows only for direct material sources of reinforcement and punishment. Social learning, on the other hand, begins with Skinner's theory and adds the concept of indirect social stimuli. Jeffery uses the more straightforward Skinnerian approach, while Akers relies on the social learning variety.

THE HERITAGE OF THE THEORY

The Social Heritage

Behavioral theories in psychology rose to the peak of their popularity in the 1960s. It was the optimistic spirit of the early part of the decade that led psychologists to believe that otherwise untreatable behavior problems could be successfully treated by using the newly developed behavioral therapies. The civil rights campaign had also spilled over into mental health issues. A recognition of the rights of mental patients gave them a right to treatment, rather than just being warehoused. Further, behavior modification, a branch of applied behavioral psychology, was especially suitable for training in life skills so that the patient could eventually be released from the institution.

As part of the "Great Society" concept, schools were experimenting with new and better ways of learning. Education began championing behavior modification and adapting it to the classroom setting. By the 1970s, people felt so convinced that behavioral psychologies were the answer to behavior problems that B. F. Skinner made the best-seller list with two popular books, *Beyond Freedom and Dignity* and *Walden II*. A futuristic movie, A *Clockwork Orange,* even featured the use of a punishment-oriented version of behavior modification.

An optimistic philosophy had also developed in corrections and the juvenile justice system, with state and federal governments funding several experimental programs. Among all of those programs, behavior modification appeared to have the most promise, largely because it seemed to work within institutions, if not outside them. Even at the end of the decade when people had become cynical about treatment programs, behavior modification programs were still in use (those versions based on punishment were, however, beginning to come under fire).

The Intellectual Heritage

The most obvious intellectual source of social learning theory is behavioristic psychology. C. Ray Jeffery adopted the approach as a faculty member at Arizona State University, where two prominent psychologists, Arthur and Carolyn Staats, were making strides in the new field of behavior modification. In addition, Jeffery was involved in the Washington, D. C., Dropout Project, a program that attempted to apply the principles of behavior modification to delinquent youth. Ronald Akers, on the other hand, developed his theory as the result of interaction with another young faculty member, Robert Burgess, in the sociology department at the University of Washington (Akers, 1985:xx). Burgess had studied behavioral psychology and convinced Akers that it could profitably be applied to criminology. Burgess was later to employ learning theory in several environmental programs, including an anti-littering program for a park system.

Perhaps as important as psychology is the heritage gained from differential association. Both Jeffery and Akers published their original learning theory articles as an explanation of Sutherland's statement, "Criminal behavior is learned." Jeffery was, in fact, one of the last of Sutherland's students. Akers, who earned his doctoral degree under Richard Quinney, was intimately familiar with Sutherland's work, especially since Quinney was working on a reformulation of differential association theory (DeFleur and Quinney, 1966).

THE THEORETICAL PERSPECTIVE

Operant and General Social Learning Theories

Before one can appreciate criminological learning theories, a basic understanding of operant-based learning theory is necessary.

Operant learning theory is concerned with the effect that an individual's behavior has on the environment and, subsequently, the consequences of that effect on the individual. As B. F. Skinner (1971:16) relates, behavior is shaped and maintained by its consequences. Therefore, behavior is a product of present and past events in the life of the individual. The contingencies of reinforcement and punishment (aversive stimuli) determine whether the frequency of any particular behavior is increased or diminished.

There are six basic principles we will discuss here: positive reinforcement, negative reinforcement, positive punishment, negative punishment, discriminative stimuli, and schedules. **Reinforcement** may be described as any event following the occurrence of behavior which alters and increases the frequency of the behavior. Some events will increase the frequency of behavior they follow. These are *positive* reinforcers, or rewards. A mother who gives her child a cookie for doing something good is providing positive reinforcement. Other events will increase the frequency of behavior if they remove something undesirable which follows the behavior. These are called *negative* reinforcers. If a child does something bad and then says that he is sorry, the mother may not punish the child. Perhaps the easiest way to distinguish between the two is that positive reinforcement provides a reward and negative reinforcement removes some form of punishment.

Punishment, or aversive stimuli, is the opposite of reinforcement. That is, it reduces the frequency of any behavior that it follows. The process of decreasing the emission of behavior through the presence of an aversive stimuli is called *positive* punishment. This is the typical reason for spanking a child. *Negative* punishment results in the removal of rewards which would ordinarily have been present after a behavior. In this case, the child does not get the cookie.

Discriminative stimuli, on the other hand, do not occur after behavior, but are present either before or as the behavior occurs. Further, they can be used to control behavior because they indicate whether reinforcement or punishment is forthcoming. Thus they function as *cues* or signals which help the individual to determine those situations in which a particular behavior may be appropriate (likely to be reinforced). It is this form of stimuli that is crucial in social settings; almost all of our social world is composed of discriminative stimuli. Advertising, for example, is nothing more than the use of discriminative stimuli to get us to associate a product with something that we find rewarding.

A final concept is that of the **schedule** of consequences. This refers to the frequency with which and probability that a particular consequence will occur, as well as the length of time it occurs after the behavior. Those consequences that immediately follow behavior and have a high probability of occurring are the ones which have the strongest effect on the individual. This means that some forms of behavior will be preferred over others because of their reinforcement schedule. Conversely, it means that if we wait too long to punish someone for a crime, for example, the punishment will lose much of its effect.

Learning, then, takes place because of the consequences associated with behavior. If an individual is reinforced after doing something, that behavior will occur again: the behavior has been learned. On the other hand, if punishment occurs after certain behavior, the individual learns to avoid that kind of behavior. Since people do not all have the same reward and punishment experiences in their past, some people will have learned some behavior while others will not have. Finally, any social environment contains several possible situations, each of which might provide different cues and consequences for a behavior. It is relatively easy to misinterpret a situation and assume that previous learning will apply when it will not.

Social learning theory also considers the concept of imitation, or **modeling**, to be central to the learning process (Bandura, 1969:118-203). This involves the process of learning by observing the behavior of others. If, for instance, some other person is rewarded for certain behavior, an individual watching that situation can learn that behavior also. In this way, the observer is "vicariously reinforced." Strict operant learning theory insists that learning must be based on behavior and consequences applied to the individual, not some other person. Therefore, social learning theory is different in that it adds the social environment to the learning process. Under this approach, it is possible to learn not only from other people around us, but also from television and movies.

Jeffery's Differential Reinforcement Theory

In 1965, C. Ray Jeffery published the first article linking criminal behavior and operant learning theory. His thesis was that differential association was "not valid in its present form, though it is basically sound in asserting that criminal behavior is learned. . . (1965:294)." Sutherland's theory needed reformulation into modern learning theory, but Jeffery maintained that once that was done the theory was no longer a theory of *social* reinforcement. It was, he said, a more complete theory which could explain how "criminal behavior can be maintained without social approval" (1965:296).

Jeffery began his theory of differential reinforcement with a brief description of the six basic operant principles above. He added one more concept to his discussion: satiation and deprivation. This concept suggests that a stimulus will be more or less reinforcing depending on the individual's current condition. For example, a person who already has wealth (satiated) will be less likely to find robbing someone of their money to be reinforcing, while the impoverished individual (deprived) will more likely see the money as a reinforcer. Such a concept of the condition of the individual allows for similar interpretations of the effect of social class and poverty as those we saw in the strain theories of Merton, Cohen, and Cloward and Ohlin.

A brief summary of the elements of differential reinforcement is as follows (Jeffery, 1965:295): People do not have the same past experiences; therefore their conditioning histories are different. The stimuli that people experience daily also have distinct meanings which produce differing qualities of reinforcement. Among these stimuli are some which have previously affected criminal behavior. Thus, some people have been reinforced for criminal behavior and some have been punished. Since most consequences are relatively intermittent (rarely is anything rewarded or punished each and every time), criminal behavior is not reinforced or punished each time it occurs. Instead, the past experience is sufficient to maintain the current criminal behavior.

Finally, Jeffery has also insisted that the most important forms of reinforcers are material, for example, money and cars. As a result, differential reinforcement maintains that one does not need associates to provide reinforcing consequences for criminal behavior, for the product of the crime itself can be the reinforcer. Other people are said to be important for their discriminative value, that is, they provide cues about the probability of being rewarded for a criminal act. This decreased emphasis on social reinforcement has continued to characterize Jeffery's work. His recent book, *Crime Prevention Through Environmental Design* (1977), incorporates his work in sociobiology and states that the reinforcing quality of all behavior lies in the brain. By this Jeffery means that the brain contains pleasure and pain centers which mediate and interpret all stimuli. Thus, he now says that social reinforcement is really a secondary form of reinforcement, and is maintained only by a relationship with the more primary form of biological reinforcement (1977:312).

Akers' Social Learning Theory

Ronald Akers and Robert Burgess provided criminology with the second connection between psychological learning theory and differential association (Burgess and Akers, 1966). After reading Jeffery's 1965 article, they decided that a more detailed statement of learning theory would be beneficial, and began the process of fully reformulating the propositions of differential association theory. The final version of seven propositions, which they labeled differential association-reinforcement theory, was not originally intended as an alternative to Sutherland's theory. However, of necessity, it became a "new, broader theory" (Akers, 1985:41).

In contrast to Jeffery's approach, it is obvious that Akers views the social environment as the most important source of reinforcement. He even suggests that most of the learning of deviant behavior is the result of social interaction (1985:45). In fact, it is the presence of various subcultures in society that allows us to predict which stimuli are likely to be effective reinforcers for people. This approach leads to the presence of *definitions* as one of the crucial aspects of the theory.

Definitions of behavior, both for Sutherland and Akers, are the moral components of social interaction which express whether something is right or wrong. Akers refers to these definitions as verbal behavior and notes that they are learned just as any other behavior is learned. Once learned, however, definitions become a form of discriminative stimuli or cues about the consequences to be expected from other behavior. They can be general, applying to a range of behavior, or specifically focused on a single form of behavior. Those that indicate approval of certain behavior are clearly positive in their action; that is, they denote that the behavior will be rewarded (positive reinforcement). Others are neutralizing definitions, providing a way to avoid some (or all) of an expected punishment, that is, negative reinforcement).

Akers has continued the development of the theory, most notably in his book, *Deviant Behavior: A Social Learning Approach* (1985). The most recent version of social learning theory retains the seven-proposition format of the original.

1.   Deviant behavior is learned according to the principles of operant conditioning.

2. Deviant behavior is learned both in nonsocial situations that are reinforcing or discriminating and through that social interaction in which the behavior of other persons is reinforcing or discriminating for such behavior.

3. The principal part of the learning of deviant behavior occurs in those groups which comprise or control the individual's major source of reinforcements.

4. The learning of deviant behavior, including specific techniques, attitudes, and avoidance procedures, is a function of the effective and available reinforcers and the existing reinforcement contingencies.

5. The specific class of behavior learned and its frequency of occurrence are a function of the effective and available reinforcers, and the deviant or nondeviant direction of the norms, rules, and definitions which in the past have accompanied the reinforcement.

6. The probability that a person will commit deviant behavior is increased in the presence of normative statements, definitions, and verbalizations which, in the process of differential reinforcement of such behavior over conforming behavior, have acquired discriminative value.

7. The strength of deviant behavior is a direct function of the amount, frequency, and probability of its reinforcement. The modalities of association with deviant patterns are important insofar as they affect the source, amount, and scheduling of reinforcement. (Ronald L. Akers, *Deviant Behavior: A Social Learning Approach,* 3rd ed. c 1985 by Wadsworth, Inc. Used by permission of the publisher.)

Social learning theory, then, states that people learn both deviant behavior and the definitions that go along with them. The learning can be direct, as through conditioning, or indirect, as through imitation and modeling. The learned deviance can then be strengthened by reinforcement or weakened by punishment. Its continued maintenance depends not only on its own reinforcement but also on the quality of the reinforcement available for alternative behavior. If the definitions of deviant behavior are reinforcing and if alternative behaviors are not reinforced as strongly, an individual is likely to engage in deviant behavior.

CLASSIFICATION OF THE THEORY

Social learning qualifies as a *positivist* theory. Compared to other theories, it focuses more directly on behavior and presents an obvious treatment of remedy for deviance. Similarly, because learning theory is so focused on the individual, it is not difficult to classify it as a *microtheory.* Even though the theoretical principles are general enough to apply to all behavior, it is a direct attempt to explain how individuals come to engage in criminal behavior.

Social learning is also a *processual* theory. It explains the process by which criminal behavior takes place and tell us why that behavior occurs. The more difficult point of classification is that of consensus-conflict. The theory itself does not require either orientation, so we must look to the theorists to determine which it is. We would infer that Jeffery takes a consensus orientation to society. This appears to be the case because his work provides many applications to "treat" criminal behavior and yet he does not question the origin of those laws which will require that treatment. In fairness to Jeffery, however, he does state that a theory of the creation of law is necessary before one can discuss criminal behavior. Akers, on the other hand, makes the statement that there is a "core of consensual values" while "admitting the importance of power and conflict" (1985:19). This, he says, is a pluralist conflict approach. Since both these theorists seem to assume a core set of common social values, however, we will classify social learning theory as a *consensus* theory.

SUMMARY

Social learning theory developed from the combination of differential association theory with psychological learning theories. Though C. Ray Jeffery's current version de-emphasizes the social aspects of learning, Akers' theory is still directly associated with Sutherland's perspective. They both, however, explain deviant behavior by emphasizing reinforcement and discriminative stimuli.

Behavior, whether deviant or not, can be expected to be maintained if it is reinforced in the social environment. Thus the problem for behavioral criminologists is to determine where these reinforcements originate. Jeffery now suggests that reinforcement is biologically based in the pleasure-pain center of the brain. Akers, preferring to keep his theory on a social level, finds the origin of deviance reinforcement in common rationalizations and in the various subcultures of society.

As has been the case for social control theory, the past decade has increased the popularity of social learning theory. However, many sociologically oriented criminologists are still skeptical of the approach because it is directly derived from psychology. Nonetheless, as one of the two major theories that does not require an acceptance of the conflict position, social learning theory has been steadily gaining in acceptance. Some theorists have even attempted to integrate social control and social learning theories (Conger, 1976), an effort Akers would seem to encourage (1985:67).

Major Points of the Theory

1. Human behavior is organized around the seeking of pleasure and the avoidance of pain.
2. The two concepts involved in the learning of behavior are reinforcement and punishment. Reinforcement increases the frequency of a behavior, whereas punishment decreases the frequency.
3. Criminal behavior is learned through both material and social reinforcements in the same way as is any other behavior. This learning process is a product of past, as well as of present, experiences; therefore, all individuals have a different set of learned behavior and expected consequences.
4. Social reinforcements serve both as factors in learning deviant behavior and in setting the values (definitions) which define behavior as good or bad, desirable or undesirable. The social environment also provides various behavior models that can be imitated.
5. Social definitions, which are originally learned in the same way as any other behavior, act as cues which signal whether a particular behavior will be reinforced or not.
6. Definitions assist in the learning of crime as direct signals that a reward is forthcoming, or as rationalizations that are used to avoid punishment for criminal behavior.
7. Criminal behavior is behavior that has been differentially reinforced through social definitions and material rewards in the individual's subcultural environment.
8. Material reinforcements are often provided by crime itself. Therefore, when individuals are deprived, criminal behavior may be maintained by its own rewards.

BIBLIOGRAPHY

ADAMS, REED L. (1973). "Differential association and learning principles revisited," *Social Problems* 20: 458–470.

AKERS, RONALD L. (1985). *Deviant Behavior: A Social Learning Approach*, 3rd ed. Belmont, CA: Wadsworth.

_____, MARVIN D. KROHN, LONN LANZA-KADUCE, and MARCIA RADOSEVICH (1979). "Social learning and deviant behavior: a specific test of a general theory," *American Sociological Review* 44: 636–55.

BANDURA, ALBERT (1969). *Principles of Behavior Modification.* New York: Holt, Rinehart and Winston.

_____ (1977). *Social Learning Theory.* Englewood Cliffs, NJ: Prentice-Hall.

BURGESS, ROBERT L., and RONALD L. AKERS (1966a). "A differential association-reinforcement theory of criminal behavior," *Social Problems* 14: 128–47.

_____, (1966b). "Are operant principles tautological?" *The Psychological Record* 16: 305–12.

BURGESS, ROBERT L., and DON BUSHELL, JR. (1969). *Behavioral Sociology: The Experimental Analysis of Social Process.* New York: Columbia University Press.

CONGER, RAND (1976). "Social control and social learning models of delinquency: a synthesis," *Criminology* 14: 17–40.

DEFLUER, MELVIN L., and RICHARD QUINNEY (1966). "A reformulation of Sutherland's differential association theory and a strategy for empirical verification," *Journal of Research in Crime and Delinquency* 3: 1–22.

HOMANS, GEORGE C. (1961). *Human Behavior: Its Elementary Forms.* New York: Harcourt, Brace & World.

JEFFERY, C. RAY (1965). "Criminal behavior and learning theory," *Journal of Criminal Law, Criminology, and Police Science* 56: 294-300.

_____ (1977). *Crime Prevention Through Environmental Design*, 2nd ed. Beverly Hills: Sage.

SKINNER, B. F. (1953). *Science and Human Behavior.* New York: Macmillan.

_____ (1971). *Beyond Freedom and Dignity.* New York: Knopf.

12

THE FUTURE OF CRIMINOLOGICAL THEORY

INTRODUCTION

One of the hazards of presenting theories one after the other is that the differences among them become magnified. Too often students (and criminologists) see the various theories as separate from each other. We have tried to show that this is really not the case by providing a brief look at the heritage of each theory. Even this, though, cannot adequately suggest the ways in which theories are related. As long as people see each theory as separate and distinct, there may be little real progress in criminology. Fortunately, there are a few people beginning to work on the integration of theories. This final chapter will discuss some of the things that have happened in criminological theory in the last fifteen years, point out the effect that we think they will have, and make some suggestions for integrating theory.

THE HERITAGE OF CONTEMPORARY THEORY

The events and influences that will affect current theoretical direction are difficult to see because of their close proximity to us. There are a few things, however, that should have a bearing on the ways that theorists are thinking. The social events are political and economic conservatism. The intellectual influences are a new discipline specializing in criminal justice and an emphasis on quantification.

Social Influences

Since the early 1970s, society has been moving in a decidedly conservative direction. With the Iranian hostage crisis, it seemed that public attitudes came together and a conservative majority opinion developed. There were political and religious factions claiming to speak for the "silent majority," an ostensibly large group of strongly religious, conservative citizens. Whether or not this silent majority exists, there has indeed been a movement toward religious fundamentalism, even to the extent of political involvement. A further impetus for this conservative direction has been the economic depression of the 1980s. Responding to fiscal necessity, many governmental programs have been cut and a pragmatic approach to expenditures in the criminal justice system has been taken.

The most important implication of this conservatist movement for criminology has been in the way that criminals are viewed. The appreciative and sympathetic portrayal of criminals in the 1960s disappeared in favor of a view of the criminal as a rational being. A rational criminal, of course, chooses to commit crimes and is not particularly amenable to expensive rehabilitative programs. Thus, other approaches are necessary. The expansion of research and literature on deterrence and just deserts exemplify the direction that many criminologists chose.

Such a focus suggests that there will be little immediate future for structural theories. The primary thrust of theory will probably be toward explaining the various processes of how one becomes criminal. These processes, given a conservative bent, will most likely be explained by emphasizing traditional values and institutions: schools, family, friends, and work. Social control theories, then, should remain popular.

The Rise of Criminal Justice

While criminology has never been the only discipline responsible for the study of crime, the years after 1965 saw the emergence of a new discipline with a singular focus on crime and the criminal justice system. This new discipline, criminal justice, arose during a period of increased federal activity in the area of crime control—mostly as a result of the 1967 President's Commission on Law Enforcement and the Administration of Justice. That commission strongly advocated that a "war against crime" be launched and that those working in the criminal justice system be professionalized. The federal agency that evolved from the work of the commission, the Law Enforcement Assistance Administration, not only spent funds to upgrade various criminal justice departments and programs but provided educational funding for college courses. Many colleges began offering criminal justice courses as a way to tap this unexpected new source of tuition funds.

The discipline of criminal justice expanded throughout the 1970s. By the end of the decade, a good portion of criminology had become part of criminal justice, with criminologists teaching and doing research within academic criminal justice departments. This movement was not without its problems, however. Between the research funding of the federal government and the practitioner-oriented focus of criminal justice departments, much of the theoretical work was left behind. The 1970s represented the only decade since 1920 in which no major new theory was developed. Theory was largely put aside in favor of pragmatic descriptions of the system and research on increasing the effectiveness of system processing. Thus, theoretical criminology suffered from a lack of creative interest. It seems reasonable to assume that there may even be some interest in building theories of the criminal justice system in lieu of continued theorizing about criminal behavior.

Quantitative Methodology and Theory

During the same period, the widespread employment of computers in criminological research assisted in the development of statistically oriented forms of data analysis. More and more attention was spent on the development of research skills and techniques, until the training of most graduate students in criminology incorporated more statistics courses than theoretical materials. This movement, in and of itself, was not particularly undesirable; extended into other areas, however, the over-emphasis on quantification represented a limited view of the world.

Since statistical analysis depends on transforming the world around us into numbers, the use of numbers often became more important than the quality of information. Mathematical formulas were developed to represent models of reality, personal characteristics were assumed from a few questions on a survey instrument, and aggregate social data were derived from the statistics collected by various governmental agencies. In short, criminologists often used data that were unsuitable to the task of conveying the complexity of life, especially where deviance was concerned. They did this, though, because those data were convenient for the statistical tools at hand.

Even this, though, did not present a particularly difficult problem for criminological theorizing. The problem here arose when quantitative methodology was extended into guidelines for theory construction. Since methodology of this type is intensely concerned with the ability to measure, the major criteria for "good" theory was that it should contain easily measured concepts. In fact, advocates of this position held that the most appropriate theory construction was a series of highly specific, objective, and mathematically formulated statements (see for instance, Dubin, 1978; Reynolds, 1971; Gibbs, 1972).

The problem with this approach is that it prevents the creation of theories about larger issues and results in a series of unconnected explanations of some very specific behavior. Many theoretical concepts are not directly measurable (for example, the notions of social structure, values, and norms which are all common to criminological literature). Further, such an approach almost precludes structural theories in favor of processual ones. This approach does, however, strongly encourage the testing of theory, and that is what the field has been doing in the last fifteen years. All of this leads us to speculate that criminologists will examine their existing data, locate relationships, and develop future theories about specific criminal behavior.

THE INTEGRATION OF THEORY

Perhaps as much as anything, criminology needs to take stock of the theories it already has. The same variables have been used time and time again to explain crime and delinquency and, yet, each time the claim was that a new theory was being developed, although not necessarily by the authors themselves. There have been some original approaches under development recently. Examples are the crime-as-self-help theory proposed by Black (1983), the routine-activity theory of Cohen and Felson (1979) and the Pepinsky and Jesilow (1985) argument for a recognition of diversity in lifestyles. None of the newer theoretical attempts have yet, however, been accepted by the field as a major departure from existing criminological theories. It may even be that we have enough theories and just need to determine what they are explaining and the context in which they work best.

At this point it makes sense to begin to determine exactly how and where existing theories fit together, something we have tried to do here by classifying each of the theories as we discussed them. Macrotheories obviously do not compete with microtheories. Structural theories may be compatible with and explain the society in which processual theories operate. Thus, a good starting point might be to integrate some of these theories.

This process of integration has already begun. We have noted that some of the theories discussed here are really integrations of two or more previous theories. Cohen, and Cloward and Ohlin, for example, integrated Chicago School approaches with the anomie tradition. The subculture of violence theory of Wolfgang and Ferracuti (1967) attempted to synthesize most of the theoretical work of its day. Recent work has focused on combining the theories of social control and social learning (Conger, 1976) or both of these with anomie theory (Elliot, Huizinga and Ageton, 1985). Even conflict and consensus versions of theory may prove to be more compatible than the field has thought (Schwendinger and Schwendinger, 1985).

CONCLUSIONS

All these different theories, and the current attempts to integrate them, often leave students of criminology puzzled. How can there be so many different explanations of the same thing, they ask. The answer lies in the fact that crime is a very complex phenomenon. Even the determination of whether behavior is criminal or not is difficult. Further, if an act occurs without the knowledge of anyone other than the perpetrator, has a crime really occurred? If a legislature passes a law which makes an act criminal, was the same act a criminal one before the passing of the law?

The sheer variety of behavior defined as criminal also presents a problem. When we use the term "crime," the reference is often to a wide range of illegal behavior. The individual criminal acts, though, may have very little in common except that someone, at some time, disliked each of them enough to have a law passed against them. Murder and petty theft, for example, have about as much in common as a rock and an orange. Thus, theories of crime and criminal behavior must encompass a wide range of human activity. This is the reason that some criminologists advocate the limiting of theories to very specific behavior.

How can these theories be used? Our answer is that they are already being used, although most people do not know they are doing so. Police departments have designed their activities around some of the theoretical explanations. Each day judges give out sentences based on their understanding of the character of the defendants and the environments in which they live. Probation officers send their clients to treatment programs to improve their work skills or to resolve their use of drugs or alcohol. Prison authorities attempt to instill discipline, teach proper work habits, and deter inmates from future criminality. Finally, as reflected in the media, the public seems to attribute criminal behavior to such things as a depressed economy, poor family life, and the influence of bad friends. Criminological theory, then, is really a part of everyday life.

BIBLIOGRAPHY

BLACK, DONALD (1983). "Crime as social control," *American Sociological Review* 48: 34–45.

COHEN, LAWRENCE E., and MARCUS FELSON (1979). "Social change and crime rates: a routine activity approach," *American Sociological Review* 44: 588–607.

CONGER, RAND (1976). "Social control and social learning models of delinquent behavior: a synthesis," *Criminology* 14: 17–40.

DUBIN, ROBERT (1978). *Theory Building*, rev. ed. New York: Free Press.

ELLIOT, DELBERT S., DAVID HUIZINGA, and SUZANNE S. AGETON (1985). *Explaining Delinquency and Drug Use.* Beverly Hills: Sage.

GIBBS, JACK P. (1972). *Sociological Theory Construction.* Hinsdale, IL: Dryden.

PEPINSKY, HAROLD E., and PAUL JESILOW (1985). *Myths That Cause Crime,* 2nd ed., annotated. Cabin John, MD: Seven Locks Press.

REYNOLDS, PAUL D. (1971). *A Primer in Theory Construction.* Indianapolis: Bobbs-Merrill.

SCHWENDINGER, HERMAN, and JULIA S. SCHWENDINGER (1985). *Adolescent Subcultures and Delinquency.* New York: Praeger.

WOLFGANG, MARVIN E., and FRANCO FERRACUTI (1967). *The Subculture of Violence: Towards an Integrated Theory in Criminology.* London: Tavistock.

INDEX

A

Abrahamsen, David, 27, 29
Adams, Reed L., 55, 127
Ageton, Suzanne S., 115, 133, 135
Aichhorn, August, 27, 29
Akers, Ronald L., 2, 9, 55, 118–19, 123–27
Allen, Francis A., 26, 30
Anderson, Nels, 44
anomie theory (*see also* strain theory, theory) 4, 8, 42, 60–67, 70–71, 75–76, 80, 98, 109, 114, 133

B

Bandura, Albert, 121, 127
Barnes, Harry E., 13, 18

Beccaria, Cesare, 12–16, 18–19
Becker, Howard S., 85–87, 89, 92
behavior modification (*see also* social learning theory, 118–19
Bentham, Jeremy, 12–16, 18–19
Bernard, Thomas J., 9, 98, 105, 110, 116
Black, Donald, 133–34
Blalock, Hubert, 3, 9
Blumer, Herbert, 47–48
Bohlander, Edward W., 101, 104
Bohm, Robert M., 101–2, 104
Bonger, William A., 97, 104
Bordua, David J., 72, 80
Briar, Scott, 112, 115
bridging theory (*see also*

theory classification), 4, 74,
76
Bulmer, Martin, 36–37, 43
Burgess, Ernest, 37, 40, 44, 49
Burgess, Robert L., 55, 119,
123, 127
Bushell, Don Jr., 127

C

capital punishment, 16–17
Chambliss, William B., 101,
104
Charon, Joel M., 44
Chicago School (*see also*
theory) 34–35, 49, 50, 70–73
76, 80, 85, 133
Chiricos, Theodore G., 55
Christiansen, Karl O., 31
Cicourel, Aaron V., 87, 93
Classical School, 6, 10–19, 22,
23, 28, 84, 102
classification (*see also* theory),
5–6
Clinard, Marshall B., 67
Cloward, Richard A., 65, 70,
75–80, 122, 133
Cohen, Albert K., 6, 55, 70,
72–76, 78–80. 111, 122, 133
Cohen, Lawrence E., 133–34
Compte, August, 25, 30
concentric zones (*see also*
ecological theory, Chicago
School, 37–38
conflict theory, (*see also*
theory), 4, 6, 78, 91, 96–105,
109, 126, 133
Conger, Rand, 115, 126–27,
133–34
containment theory (*see also*
social control theory) 114

context of theory, 7–8
intellectual, 7, 14–15,
23–24, 36, 49–50, 61–62,
71–72, 85, 97, 109–10 119
social, 7, 12–13, 22–23,
34–35, 48–49, 60–61,
70–71, 84–85, 96–97,
108–9, 118–19
Coser, Lewis, 97, 104
Cressey, Donald R., 48, 50–52,
54–57
Cressey, Paul F., 35, 44
crime, definition of, 134
Cullen, Francis T., 76, 81
Culture conflict theory, 40–43,
50, 51
primary conflict, 41
secondary conflict, 41

D

Dahrendorf, Ralf, 97, 104
Davis, Nanette J., 8
Debro, Julius, 86–87, 92
definition of the situation (*see
also* symbolic
interactionism, 39–40, 42,
52–53
Defleur, Melvin L., 56, 119,
127
determinism, 22, 28, 42
deterrence, 12, 14–16, 18, 28,
120–21, 131
deviance amplification (*see
also* labeling theory), 88
Dietrick, David C., 72, 81
differential association-
reinforcement theory (*see*
social learning theory)
differential association theory
(*see also* theory), 3, 48–57,

76, 79, 114, 119, 121, 123, 125

differential reinforcement theory (*see* social learning theory)

differential opportunity theory (*see also* theory, subculture theories) 4, 75, 78, 98

Dinitz, Simon, 111, 115–16

division of labor, 60–62

drift theory (*see also* social control theory), 112

Driver, Edwin A., 30

Dubin, Robert, 3, 9, 67, 132, 134

Dugdale, Richard L., 27, 30

Durkheim, Emile, 30, 36, 60–62, 67, 109–10, 112, 115

E

Edgerton, Robert, 36, 44

Elliot, Delbert S., 115, 133, 135

Empey, Lamar T., 108, 115

epidemiology, 4

empiricism, 2–3, 34

Erikson, Kai T., 92

etiology, 5, 53

evolution, 22–24

F

false consciousness, 101

Farrel, Ronald A., 8, 98, 104

Farris, Robert E. L., 37, 44

feeblemindedness, 3, 27, 49

Felson, Marcus, 133–34

Ferracuti, Franco, 70, 79, 81, 133, 135

Ferri, Enrico, 26, 30

Fletcher, Ronald, 25, 30

focal concerns (*see also* subculture theories), 70, 78

free will, 12, 15, 17–18, 22

Friedlander, Kate, 27, 30

functionalism, 65, 71

G

gangs, 70–79
  conflict, 76, 78
  criminal, 76–77
  retreatist, 76–77

Garfinkel, Harold, 88, 92

Garofalo, Raffaele, 26–27, 29–30

Geis, Gilbert, 19

Gibbons, Don C., 6, 8–9, 50, 98, 104

Gibbs, Jack P., 3, 6, 9. 132, 135

Glaser, Daniel, 56

Glueck, Eleanor, 27, 30

Glueck, Sheldon, 27, 30, 56

Goddard, Henry H., 27, 30

Goffman, Erving, 92

Gold, Martin, 2, 9, 56

Gordon, David M., 101, 104

Goring, Charles B., 27, 30

Gould, Leroy C., 56

Gove, Walter R., 87, 93

Greenberg, David R., 97, 101, 104

Guerry, Andre M., 25, 28, 30

H

Halfpenny, Peter, 24, 30

Harary, Frank, 67

Hathaway, Starke R., 27, 30

Healey, William, 27, 31

hedonism, 14–15, 17, 72
Hegel, Georg W. F., 97
Heredity, 27, 36, 38, 49
Hirschi, Travis, 65, 67,
    108–10, 112–13, 115, 118
Homans, George C., 127
Hooton, Ernest A., 27, 30
Howard, John, 13, 16, 19
Hughes, Everett C., 89, 93
Huizinga, David, 115, 133, 135

I

illegitimate opportunity
    structure, 75–77
imitation, 27, 121, 124
immigration, 34–35, 37–38, 40,
    49–50
integrated community, 71–72,
    75–77
integrated theory, 8, 133
interactionism, (*see* symbolic
    interaction)

J

Jeffery, C. Ray, 12, 19, 27, 31,
    48, 56, 118–19, 121–23, 125,
    127
Jesilow, Paul, 101, 104, 133,
    135

K

Kant, Immanuel, 13, 19
Kaplan, Howard, 31
Kitsuse, John, I., 72, 81, 87, 93
Kobrin, Solomon, 35, 44, 71,
    75, 81

Kornhauser, Ruth R., 6, 9
Krohn, Marvin D., 127

L

labeling theory (*see also*
    theory) 3, 40, 84–93, 96–97,
    109
Lange, Hohannes, 27, 31
Lanza–Kaduce, Lonn, 127
Laub, John, 35, 40, 44, 71, 81
Law Enforcement Assistance
    Administration (LEAA), 131
Lemert, Edwin M., 85, 89–90,
    93
level of explanation, 4–5,
Lewis, J. David, 44
life history, 34, 37–38, 49–50
Lindesmith, Alfred, 49, 55
Locke, John, 14, 19
Lofland, John, 93
Lombroso, Cesare, 26, 31

M

macrotheory (*see also* theory
    classification), 4, 17, 28, 42,
    65, 76, 102, 133
Maestro, Marcello T., 13, 15,
    19
Mannheim, Hermann, 19,
    30–31
Marx, Karl, 97, 101
master status, (*see also*
    labeling theory), 89–90
Matza, David, 34, 44, 91, 93,
    109, 111–13, 115
McKay, Henry D., 36, 38, 42,
    45, 49–50, 56–57, 61, 72
McKenzie, Roderick D., 44

Mead, George H, 39, 42, 44, 49, 85
Mednick, Sarnoff A., 27, 31–32
Merton, Robert K., 60–67, 70–72, 75–77, 80, 122
Michalowski, Raymond J., 101, 104
microtheory, 4, 28, 42, 53, 90, 114, 125, 133
middle-class measuring rod (*see also* subculture theory), 72–73
Miller, Walter B., 70, 78–79, 81
modes of adaptation (*see also* anomie theory) 63–66
    conformity, 63, 66
    innovation, 63, 66
    rebellion, 64, 66
    retreatism, 64, 66, 76–77
    ritualism, 63–64, 66
mode of production (*see also* conflict theory), 101–2
Monachesi, Elio D., 19, 27, 30
Montesquieu, Charles L., 14–15, 19
Murray, Ellen, 116

N

Nettler, Gwynn, 6, 9, 41, 44
Nisbet, Robert A., 8–9
Nye, F. Ivan 2, 10, 85, 93, 109, 115

O

official statistics, 25, 34, 36–37, 48–49, 61, 85, 87

Ohlin, Lloyd, E., 70, 75–80, 133
Olsen, Marvin, 60, 67
operant learning theory, 118–19, 121–23
Orcutt, James D., 6, 9, 87, 93

P

Park, Robert E., 37, 40, 44, 49
Parsons, Talcott, 61–62, 67, 71
Pepinski, Harold E., 101, 104, 133, 135
personality, 27, 31, 108, 110–11
phrenology, 25
Piliavin, Irving, 112, 116
Platt, Tony, 101, 104
Positive School, 6, 21–32
positivism (*see also* theory classification), 22–28, 30–31, 36, 42, 49
    definition, 24
    logical, 24

Q

qualitative methodology, 3
quantitative methodology, 3, 132
Quetelet, Adolpne, 25, 28, 31
Quinney, Richard, 56, 97, 101–2, 105, 119, 127

R

Radosevich, Marcia, 127
Rauschenbush, Winifred, 45
reaction-formation (*see also* subculture theories), 73–74

Reckless, Walter C., 109, 111, 115–16
Reid, Sue Titus, 6, 9
Reiss Jr., Albert J., 2, 9, 45, 109–11, 116
retrospective interpretation (see also labeling theory), 89–90
Reynolds, Paul D., 132, 135
Rhodes, A. Lewis, 2, 9
Rothman, David, 23, 31
routine-activity theory, 133

S

Samenow, Stanton E., 27, 32
Savitz, Leonard D., 24, 31
Schafer, Stephen, 25, 31
Schrag, Clarence, 56, 81
Schuessler, Karl, 49–50, 53, 55–56
Schwendinger, Herman, 101, 105, 133, 135
Schwendinger, Julia, 101, 105, 133, 135
science, 14, 22, 36
secondary deviance (see also labeling theory) 89–92
self concept, 39, 42, 89, 92, 111
self-help theory, 133
self-report studies, 2, 85, 110
Sellin, Thorsten, 31, 40–41, 44–45, 49–50, 56
Shaw, Clifford, R., 36, 38, 42, 44, 49–50, 57, 61, 72
Shelden, William H., 27, 31
Short, James F., Jr., 2, 5, 9, 36, 45, 85, 93, 112, 116
Simmel, Georg, 97
Skinner, B. F., 118, 120, 127
Smith, Richard L., 19
Snodgrass, Jon, 45, 50, 57

social contract, 14, 18
social control theory (see also theory), 4, 106–16, 126, 131, 133
attachment, 112–13
belief, 113
commitment, 112–13
involvement, 113
social disorganization, 38, 42–44, 51–52, 62, 66, 77, 114
social learning theory (see also theory), 4, 118–27, 133
Sorokin, Pitirim, 61, 67
Spitzer, Steven, 101–2, 105
Staats, Arthur, 119
statistics, 132
status-frustration (see also subculture theories), 72–74
strain theory, 6, 42, 64, 73–74, 76, 109, 122
Strodtbeck, Fred L., 112, 116
subculture theories (see also theory), 4, 70–80, 98, 109, 133
delinquent, 72, 78
violence, 79
Sutherland, Edwin H., 40, 45, 48–57, 61, 70–72, 119, 121, 123, 125, 127
Swigert, Victoria L., 8, 98, 104
Sykes, Gresham M., 98, 105, 109, 111–12, 116
symbolic interactionism (see also Chicago School, labeling theory), 38–40, 42, 49–50, 54, 84–85, 91

T

Tannenbaum, Frank, 86, 93
Tarde, Gabriel, 27, 31

Taylor, Ian, 9, 105
techniques of neutralization
(*see also* social control
theory), 111–13
Terzola, Dennis A., 57
theory, 2–8, 131–34
 classification, 5–6
  classical, 6, 90, 102
  conflict, 6, 17, 42, 54, 78,
   90, 102, 125
  consensus, 6, 17, 42, 54,
   78, 90,. 102, 125
  positivist, 6, 28, 42, 53,
   64, 74, 76, 90, 113, 125
  processual, 6, 28, 42, 54,
   73, 76, 90, 113, 125,
   132
  structural, 6, 17, 54, 65,
   73, 76, 90, 102, 131–33
 construction, 132–33
 criteria for, 3, 132
 definition, 2
 major points, 18, 29, 43–44,
  54–55, 65–66, 74–75,
  77–78, 91–92, 103–4,
  114–15, 126
Thomas, William I., 37, 39–40,
 42, 45, 49, 85
Thrasher, Frederic, 45
Tifft, Larry L., 100, 105
Toby, Jackson, 112, 116
Turk, Austin T., 97, 99–100,
 105

U

utilitarianism, 12

V

Vasoli, Robert H., 57
Vold, George B., 9, 49, 57, 96,
 99, 105, 110, 116
Volkman, Rita, 57
Voltaire, Francois, 15, 19

W

Walton, Paul, 9, 105
Weber, Max, 97
Whyte, William F., 35, 45
Wilkins, Leslie T., 88, 93
Williams III, Frank P., 5, 7,
 10, 105, 116
Wirth, Louis, 40, 45, 50
Wolfgang, Marvin E., 32, 70,
 79, 81, 133, 135

Y

Yochelson, Samuel, 2, 32
Young, Jock, 9, 105

Z

Zorbaugh, Frederick, 45